VIENNA

GOOD STORIES REVEAL as much, or more, about a locale as any map or guidebook. Whereabouts Press is dedicated to publishing books that will enlighten a traveler to the soul of a place. By bringing a country's stories to the English-speaking reader, we hope to convey its culture through literature. Books from Whereabouts Press are essential companions for the curious traveler, and for the person who appreciates how fine writing enhances one's experiences in the world.

"Coming newly into Spanish, I lacked two essentials—a childhood in the language, which I could never acquire, and a sense of its literature, which I could."

—Alastair Reid, *Whereabouts: Notes on Being a Foreigner*

OTHER TRAVELER'S LITERARY COMPANIONS

Amsterdam	*Ireland*
Australia	*Israel*
Chile	*Italy*
China	*Japan*
Costa Rica	*Mexico*
Cuba	*Prague*
France	*Spain*
Greece	*Vietnam*

FORTHCOMING:

Argentina	*South Africa*
Brazil	*Poland*
India	*Turkey*

VIENNA

A TRAVELER'S LITERARY COMPANION

EDITED BY

DONALD G. DAVIAU

WHEREABOUTS PRESS
BERKELEY, CALIFORNIA

FIBER USED IN THIS PRODUCT LINE
MEETS THE SOURCING REQUIREMENTS
OF THE SFI PROGRAM
WWW.SFIPROGRAM.ORG

Published by
Whereabouts Press
Berkeley, California
www.whereaboutspress.com

Distributed to the trade by PGW / Perseus Distribution

Map courtesy of Freytag-Berndt u. Artaria, 1231 Vienna

MANUFACTURED IN THE UNITED STATES OF AMERICA

Library of Congress Cataloging-in-Publication Data
Vienna : a traveler's literary companion /
edited by Donald G. Daviau.
p.   cm. — (Travelers literary companions ; 17)
ISBN-13: 978-1-883513-10-8 (alk. paper)
1. Short stories, Austrian—Translations into English.
2. Austrian fiction—21st century—Translations into English.
3. Vienna—Fiction. I. Daviau, Donald G.

5 4 3 2 1

Contents

Preface

Thousand-year-old Austria has lived through a turbulent and colorful history, and much of it has been preserved and can still be viewed today throughout the land but nowhere more than in Vienna. The country was founded to serve as a buffer to keep invaders from the east and south from attacking Germany, a role that it performed valiantly in the sixteenth and seventeenth centuries against the Turks. In the nineteenth century, the wall around the inner city of Vienna was razed and replaced by the acclaimed Ringstrasse, which was lined with such impressive buildings as the University of Vienna, the Burgtheater, the Art Museum, the Natural History Museum, the Imperial Palace and the Opera House, each in a historical style that matches its function. Well-kept spacious parks and lavish palace gardens, all in close proximity, added to these sights. Within the Ringstrasse one is surrounded by history.

After decades of being reduced to a small portion of its former Habsburg self, Austria's fortunes took a major turn for the better with the formation of the European Union, which has brought prosperity, closer ties with Germany and with most of the former Habsburg states, and an end to the nagging and much-debated question of Austrian identity, as the country becomes increasingly European in outlook. Much of Viennese literature grapples with the issue of identity. Two years ago Austria created the first literary prize for a book by any member of the European Union. There had been voices in Austria since the 1920s advocating a united Europe with Vienna as the center because of its geographical location at the heart of Europe, making it a natural bridge between east and west and north and south, but this suggestion was not followed.

Vienna, which once served as a Roman encampment (as the excavation on the Minoritenplatz on view in the center of the city documents), has developed differently than the rest of the country because of the masses of Eastern Europeans, who, beginning in the 1880s, flocked to the magnetic flourishing city, lured by the prospect of jobs and a better life. By 1900 Vienna had the largest Czech population of any city, including Czechoslovakia itself (Franz Kafka's inclusion in this collection is a literary reflection of this). The city is known as Red (liberal) Vienna as traditionally opposed to the Black (conservative) provinces. In recent years, however, Styria, Burgenland, and Salzburg have broken ranks and adopted a socialist outlook and think and operate more like Vienna. Since the nineteenth century, Vienna has served as a mecca for tourists, fascinated by this attractive city, rich in historical atmosphere and warm in hospitality. Apart from a few modern buildings like the Hochhaus, the inner city, dominated by Vienna's main landmarks, the imposing Gothic St. Stephen's Cathedral from the twelfth century, the Graben with its highly ornate baroque statue commemorating the deadly plague in the seventeenth century, and the entrance to the grounds of the imperial palace flanked by its guardian statues and featuring the impressive iron grill over the entryway on Michaelerplatz . . . all remain as they have been for hundreds of years. A vigilant government carries on an active program of restoration and preservation, as it strives to protect Vienna's historical appearance. Buildings in the inner city may be modernized on the inside, but the original facades must remain unchanged.

Many tourists never stray far away from the inner city because of the number and variety of museums, theaters, operas, coffee houses, restaurants, and stores, except to take the D-streetcar to Belvedere Palace to see the important Museum of Modern Art or the number 38 from Schottentor to Grinzing to sample the vintage Austrian wines in the atmosphere of the old wine houses. From Grinzing one can also take a bus up to the Kahlenberg, where one has a spectacular view of Vienna and can also hike in the Vienna Woods. There are commercial day and evening tours that in addition to the sightseeing in the city include a stop at a wine house in Grinzing, where one may wine and dine, possibly with the accompaniment of some zither music. The selection here by Ingeborg Bachmann humorously satirizes such a tour and the inadequacies of the guide in language and knowledge. For another trip one can take the subway (Vienna features one of the most efficient mass-transit systems you will find anywhere) to Hietzing to see Schönbrunn, the former imperial summer palace with its extensive, manicured grounds and the prominent Gloriette on the hill as an imposing backdrop. From the subway station one will see the Park Hotel, where Mark Twain, who loved Vienna, lived for two years.

Viennese, whose identity is largely shaped by their political affiliation and the Catholic Church, have not always been kind to outsiders. They persecuted Protestants in the seventeenth century, made the Czechs and other Easterners feel unwelcome in the nineteenth century, and throughout their history have always displayed some degree of anti-Semitism. Today the climate of intolerance has not disappeared entirely but it has improved. The government finally apologized for the country's role in the Holocaust, and in recent years Austria has done more than any other European country to provide a haven for many asylum seekers from Eastern nations and also from Africa to add to the mix of former Turkish and Yugoslav guest workers who did not wish to return home. The ethnic diversity of the population will increase in future years because people from all of the member nations of the European Union may now move to any country to live, study, and seek employment, and Vienna remains a magnet.

Vienna has become one of the most successful cities in Europe in terms of business and finance, but not at the expense of its role as a center of culture. One of its first actions after World War II, when Austria was devastated and then occupied, was to renovate and reopen the theaters and the opera as a means of uplifting the spirits of the people. The nation has always turned to its literary and cultural heritage to draw strength in difficult times. After 1945 Otto Basil with his journal, *Plan*, worked to revitalize literature by reconnecting to the tradition that had been interrupted in 1938 by the German annexation. No noteworthy Austrian literature appeared during the war years, except ironically that produced by the Jewish writers in exile, who continued to produce important works while living for the day they could return home.

In the 1950s the returned exile author Hans Weigel began gathering and encouraging the numerous young writers with new themes and modern techniques. An enlightened government recognized the importance of literature and the other arts to the country and adopted a cultural policy to provide financial support to writers and artists in every field, a program that continues unabated today. For that reason Austria has many more writers than would be expected in a land of its size and has remained the leading German-speaking literature to the present day. Authors may receive a subsidy to write a book, which the state pays to have published and officially presented. No writer can live on the income from his or her books, not even the leading Austrian author, Peter Handke, whose literary papers the Government recently purchased so that he will have money to live on in retirement. To help authors survive, they are paid for lectures and for readings from their works, subsidized for reading tours, at times in foreign countries, and ultimately granted a pension in their old age. The theaters, operas, and the radio station ORF are also heavily subsidized, as are such literary organizations as Die alte Schmiede, Die Gesellschaft fuer Literatur, and the Literaturhaus, each of which offers the public several presentations—literary lectures, readings by authors and exhibits—every week without any admission charge.

Because of the close relationship of Austria and Germany up to 1804, distinctly Austrian literature only began to appear in the nineteenth century. Franz Grillparzer proclaimed independence in 1832 when he declared he was an Austrian, not a German author. The unique character of Austrian literature is henceforth readily apparent, particularly in the plays of Ferdinand Raimund and Johann Nestroy, authors who have no counterparts in German literature. Other notable nineteenth-century writers of note include the poet Nikolaus von Lenau, who attempted a new life in Ohio but returned home because of ill health, and the remarkable Charles Sealsfield, who emigrated to the United States and became a noted author of books about the western expansion. He wrote in English and critics, thinking he was an American, praised his writings as superior to those of James Fenimore Cooper.

Up to 1848, under the rule of Emperor Franz I and his loyal Chancellor Metternich, there was no freedom of speech or press in Austria because of the fear instilled in the emperor by the French revolution of 1789. He dedicated his rule to stifling progress and maintaining the status quo. He did not want enlightened citizens but obedient subjects of the state. Even the universities were prohibited from engaging in research. After the revolution of 1848, the new young emperor Franz Josef I was persuaded to tear down the old city wall that prevented expansion of the inner city and construct the showcase of buildings and palaces along the Ringstrasse. By around 1900, writers and all other artists and intellectuals contributed to implementing the program of modernity, devised and publicized by the author Hermann Bahr, the movement that ushered Austria as well as the eastern states into the twentieth century.

Life was grand in this heady atmosphere of what author Stefan Zweig called "the golden age of security," that is, if you were titled, wealthy, or talented. The turn of the century, or as it is often called, *fin-de-siècle* Vienna, remains one of the most glamorous, exciting, and significant periods of Austrian literary, cultural, and scientific history, a flowering that rivals the Renaissance in its scope and importance, radiating from Austria in all directions. Much of the thinking shaping societies today — the independent lifestyle, the belief that each individual should be free to develop to the fullest—and a number of scientific developments were introduced during this uniquely fertile era, which gave birth to the unstoppable dynamic modern spirit animating, driving, and transforming societies from the stagnant nineteenth to the explosive twentieth century. The dramatic changes that took place in Europe during the second half of the nineteenth century—the rapid expansion of industrialization and the concomitant shift from a primarily agrarian to an urban society, the breakthroughs and advances in the sciences, the change from a belief in absolute to relative values, the replacement of the aristocracy by the monied bourgeoisie as the dominant economic and political class, and the gaining of voting privileges that propelled the move to democratization—acted as a catalyst for the "transformation of all values" (Nietzsche) during the transitional years, which lasted up to the outbreak of World War I in 1914.

One of the greatest social changes has been in the status of women, who are still struggling to achieve full parity in the patriarchal society, including equal pay with men. Great improvement has been made, especially in the arts, where acknowledgment is based on ability rather than gender. When the noblewoman Marie von Ebner-Eschenbach began to write in the nineteenth century, an attempt was made to discourage her by insisting that such activity was unseemly for a woman. Because of her status she could ignore the warnings and persevere to become one of Austria's greatest authors. Today outstanding women writers are well represented in the upper echelon of important authors, and all have received the same recognition in terms of support, awards, and prizes. Elfriede Jelinek's "The Lovers," included in this collection, is an apt representation of literature's reflection of this feminist change.

Great literature aims to convey information and provide entertainment, and this collection of short prose writings by a small representative sample of the leading Viennese authors of the last hundred years is intended to fulfill that goal. These stories reflect the lifestyles, attitudes, and interpersonal relationships of a constantly developing society. As might be expected in the land that produced Freud, Viennese authors often focus on the inner life of the characters, portraying how they live or fail to fully live and how in terms of their nature, character, and background they react to an unexpected occurrence or circumstance in their lives. Thomas Bernhard, whose "Woodcutters" is included in this anthology, is a perfect example of an author whose work focuses on the thorough exploration of the inner human condition. Up to 1945 Austrian writers, including all the major authors in exile, focused their attention almost exclusively on Vienna. Only after the war, because of the Four Power Occupation and exiles who returned with expanded horizons, did the authors begin to range more widely in their choice of themes. Contributing importantly to this broadening was the influx of American and British literature and cinema.

Austrian literature has a global reach today, and it is particularly no stranger to the United States. At the turn of the century the plays of Bahr, Hofmannsthal, and Schnitzler, among others, were regularly performed on New York stages in German and in English, while the works of other authors were regularly translated. In the late 1920s, to speed up its development and at the same time to eliminate competition, Hollywood began aggressively recruiting talented writers, actors, actresses, directors, and cameramen from Austria, which had been instrumental in developing the film business. This influx of professionals was augmented significantly in the 1930s with the rush of exiled artistic talent, a veritable Who's Who of authors, musicians, and artists, fleeing from the threat of Hitler's annexation of Austria. In the United States, however, Austrians have never promoted themselves or featured their nationality and so their accomplishments gain no recognition for their country. They are *The Quiet Invaders*, as G. Wilder Spaulding titled his book describing the many contributions they have made to their host country. Writers in particular often go unnoticed as Austrians because of the tendency of American publishers to identify everything written in the German language as German literature.

The focus of this volume on Vienna and the space limitation prevented the inclusion of some of the most important contemporary authors, whose work deals with other areas of Austria, or appear in the form of poetry or plays. This brief collection is only the tip of the iceberg. If this introduction appeals to you, I urge you to further pursue the writings of Ilse Aichinger, Peter Handke, Marlen Haushofer, Robert Menasse, Anna Mitgutsch, Felix Mitterer, Christoph Ransmayr, Elisabeth Reichart, and Peter Turrini. The books of these authors can all be found in English translation. From the beginning of the nineteenth century to the present, every writer of importance is represented in English, in some cases by one or two works; in many others by their complete works. In the meantime, whether you are visiting this city that I love and have come to call my second home—or you are at home in the comfort of your armchair—I hope that this companion of Viennese authors provides you a window into the rich world of Austrian literature, and into the hearts and minds of the Viennese themselves.

Donald G. Daviau
July 2008

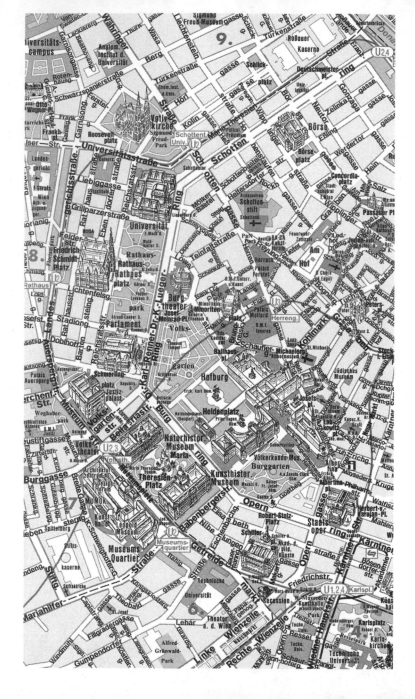

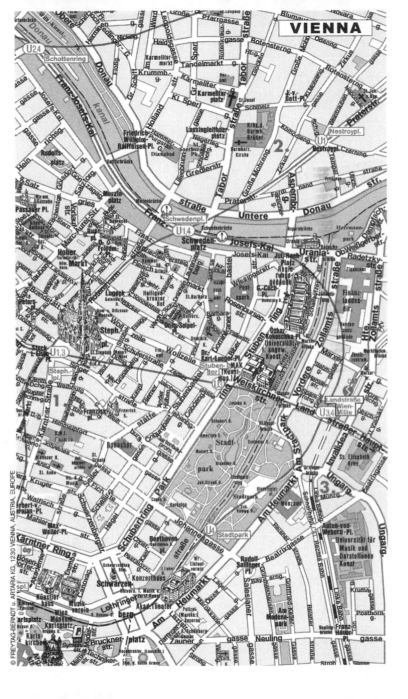

VIENNA

Sightseeing in an Old City

Ingeborg Bachmann

BECAUSE MALINA AND I want to see the Vienna we've
never seen before, we take a tour with the AUSTROBUS.
The tour guide hangs a Beethoven mask around his neck,
and while we experience a whole new Vienna according
to the views of a travel agency we know nothing about, he
concerns himself with speaking English for the Americans, looking mistrustfully only at us, even though we

---

INGEBORG BACHMANN (born in Klagenfurt in 1926–
died in Rome in 1973), with a background of philosophy and
psychology, rose to fame as one of the illustrious postwar generation of writers in Austria. She never married, and because
of her lifestyle as an adventurous artist she became an icon for
feminists. In 1953 she moved to Rome, where she died pre-
maturely in a fire in her bedroom. Her enduring reputation is
based on her prose narratives, essays, and dramas. Like other
Austrian authors, one of Bachmanns's early concerns was to
restore precise meaning to language, which had suffered from
its misuse in Nazi propaganda. Her most important theme
deals with individuals at a crossroads in their lives, trying to
decide whether to continue the imperfect, unsatisfying life
they are leading or make a change. Widely translated, she is
represented in English by the novel *Malina* and two collections
of prose tales *The Thirtieth Year* and *Three Paths to the Lake.*

I

registered as Mr. and Mrs. Malina so we could travel
with real foreigners. The tour guide has probably traveled
through Vienna with all kinds of foreigners—Brazilians,
Pakistanis, and Japanese—because otherwise he couldn't
allow himself these daring digressions and stops at the
strangest places. Because to begin with, for example, the
man only allows stops at a lot of fountains; everyone may
get off and drink from the Fountain of Geniuses, the
Danubius Fountain, and even from the Liberation of the
Spring Fountain in the City Park. The tour guide declares
that everyone has to have drunk Viennese mountain spring
water, *the most famous water in the world,* at least once.
Without any stops, the tour continues past many gray-
green baroque domes, skipping the Karlskirche, leaving
out the National Library, and on the mountain face of
St. Martin's, Archduke Charles, the victor, the lion of
Aspern is mixed up with the Emperor Maximilian the
First, whom an angel saved from a Tyrolean mountain
face after he lost his bearings and whom the tour guide
without hesitation set on a horse to Vienna. To Malina's
and my astonishment, the tour stops in front of a confec-
tionery shop in the inner city: the Americans have five
minutes to buy Mozartkugeln, the most famous Austrian
chocolates, ad gloriam and in memoriam *of the most famous
composer of all the times,* and while the Americans obe-
diently bite into a dried-out imitation of Mozartkugeln
from Salzburg, we circle the monument commemorating
the plague, *to remember the most famous and dreadful illness
in the world which was stopped with the Austrian forces and
the prayers of Emperor Leopold I.* We drive quickly past the
State Opera House, *where are happening the greatest sing-*

ing successes and singing accidents in the world, then drive particularly fast past the Burgtheater, *where are happening every evening the old and most famous dramas and murderings in Europa.* The tour guide runs out of breath in front of the university, hastily declaring it *the oldest museum of the world* and then, relieved, points to the Votive Church, *which was built to remember the salvation from the first turkish danger and the beaten turks left us the best coffee and the famous viennese breakfast* Kipfel, *to remember.* He whispers to the driver, with whom he's in cahoots, and out of the city we drive. Then because of the possibility of something collapsing we have to avoid the Stephansdom, the mammoth Pummerin Bell had just been loaned to America to be shown in a traveling exhibition, the giant ferris wheel is unfortunately under reconstruction at one of the big German firms, being made bigger for future, bigger and bigger demands. Our dear Lord is pointed to in passing; he has a peaceful bench in the Lainzer Tiergarten Park. At Schönbrunn Palace a rest stop is finally made, and everyone shyly admires the Doppelganger of the emperor of peace, who, his seventieth anniversary of governing behind him, walks solitary and dignified through the park. He didn't want it. He was spared nothing. The tour guide leafs through his notes, finally finding the passage: "to my peoples!" Already suspecting, the tour guide looks at Malina and me for help, because he doesn't seem to know how to translate these three words. But Malina looks at him, unmoved. The tour guide asks: *is something wrong, Sir?* Malina smiles and answers in his best English: *Oh, no, it's extremely interesting, I'm interested in history, I love culture, I adore such old countries like yours.*

The tour guide loses his suspicion, switches into another sentence: *Wednesday, July 29, 1914, the Emperor of the most famous Empire in the world spoke to his nineteen peoples and declared that in the most earnest hour of the greatest decision of our time before the Almighty, he is conscious.* A petite miss exclaims, "Gosh!" She doesn't want to believe that such a small country was once a big country; she was prepared for an operetta, for Grinzing, for the beautiful blue Danube. Our tour guide sets the pretty little American straight: *This was the biggest country which ever existed in the world and it gave a famous word, in the country the sun never goes down.* Malina says helpfully: "the sun never set."

But soon it's peaceful again, an anarchist killed Ms. Romy Schneider, in Korfu and in Miramar conference participants are in session at countless conferences, and Madeira is booming due to cruise trips. The tour guide turns tenderhearted, indulging himself in the dream of a waltz, the white lilacs are blooming again and in the Prater the trees are blooming again; Crown Prince Rudolf becomes acquainted with Madame Catherine Deneuve, who thank God is known to everyone in the AUSTRO-BUS. In Mayerling we stand around in the rain, the strictest order of nuns guards over a small wash stand that is permitted to be exhibited; there aren't any blood stains because the wing that contained this room was, by order of the Emperor, torn down a half century ago and replaced with a chapel. Only one nun is allowed to speak with us; all the other nuns pray for her, intercede for her. Night comes upon us suddenly. We haven't gotten everything for our money yet, "Vienna by night is still ahead." At the first tavern the gypsy barons and Csardas princesses appear and are enthusiastically applauded, there are two glasses of wine for everyone, in the second tavern the long-haired beggar-students are lounging around and the bird peddlers go yodeling from table to table, there's a glass of German sparkling wine for everyone, the Americans are growing more and more spirited, we continue through the inner city from one land of smiles to another, an older American, overly enthusiastic, harasses the merry widow. At 5 A.M. we all sit before a goulash soup, including the driver from the AUSTROBUS. The tour guide offers the petite miss the Beethoven mask in a gesture of reconciliation, and everyone sings "Tales from the Vienna Woods," the tour guide and bus driver attempt "Vienna Life" alone. Finally it becomes apparent that only the driver really has a splendid voice, and everybody wants him to sing solo —there's no holding back for him. "Vienna, City of My Dreams!" Malina is exhausted, and I sense the feeling passing to me, he slides a tip to the driver who winks at me, the only one who has seen through me—he won't let me out of his sight, doesn't pay one bit of attention to the American girl, and sings to Malina: Give the laughing, charming women in Beauuutiful Vienna my greetings! *Your husband doesn't like music?* the tour guide asks with concern, and I, confused, tell him: *not so late, not so early in the morning.* Malina begins talking overanimatedly to the older American, he pretends to teach European history at a midwestern university, he's so surprised by his first stay in Vienna, there's so much to notice here that's never been noticed before, like how Western Civilization is being saved here in every place, here there is still this legendary tradition, movie theaters are dedicated to Apollo, Thalia,

Eos, Urania, the Phoenix, yes indeed even to the cosmos, Eden is even a nightclub, a mild, filter cigarette for women advertises for Diana, Memphis is called to mind by the competition. I think about our apostolic emperors and whisper to Malina: I think the man just doesn't dare say that they've been baked into Kaiser rolls and shredded into Kaiserschmarrn. The American, who confesses to be a Missourian, toasts Malina, recognizing in him a *fine guy* who will take his observations and knowledge over the big pond into the wilderness.

Strengthened by the goulash soup and songs, the tour guide remembers that it's not yet time for bed, but that the tour continues unmercifully, because it's already bright outside.

Ladies and Gentlemen! Our trip will finish in the Kapuzinergruft. The Americans look at each other questioningly and disappointedly. Some would rather go to the Prater, but mornings there's no Prater and no wine taverns either, and we've already stopped in front of the Kapuziner Church and have to enter the crypt, fatigued and chilly. *Here you call see the most famous collection in the world, the hearts of all the Habsburgian emperors and empresses, archdukes and archduchesses.* A drunk old American woman starts laughing, the petite miss drops the Beethoven mask and shouts, *Gosh!* We all want to get out of the crypt, the older American who still liked the merry widow throws up. The tour guide is scandalized and curses, but no longer in English—foreigners are only out for a good time, are clueless about culture, show no respect, his job has to be the most thankless in the world, no pleasure whatsoever guiding these hordes of barbarians through Viennese days and nights. He drives his herd back into the bus. Malina and I don't board, we offer our thanks and claim to be only a few steps from our hotel, go silently, arm-in-arm, to the next taxi stand, pressing tightly against one another. We don't say a word in the taxi, Malina's about to fall asleep, and home in the Ungargasse I say: that was your idea after all. Malina says exhaustedly, I beg your pardon, that was once again your idea.

Translated by Margaret McCarthy

Visit to Vienna

Erich Wolfgang Skwara

THE WINDOW FACES the *Musikverein,* and behind that
rises the cupola of the St. Charles Church, green and at
peace with the broad sky. The towers, really columns, are
there too, topped by imperial orbs or crowns. They can't
be discerned at this distance, and that doesn't mean anything either. The main thing is that he has slept well and
the sun is shining.

ERICH WOLFGANG SKWARA (born in Salzburg in
1948) studied music history and French literature in Paris and
completed his Ph.D at the State University of New York at
Albany. He holds dual citizenship in Austria and the United
States. He taught at the University of Maryland, at George-
town University, and since 1986 has been professor of Humani-
ties and Comparative Literature at San Diego State University,
where he divides the year teaching and traveling. Skwara knew
that he wanted to be a writer from the age of seven when he
published his first poem in a newspaper, and along with countless short texts in newspapers and literary magazines he has
written seven novels and seven volumes of poetry. He avoids
political topics but devotes himself to examinations of life as
manifested in the feelings of the transitory nature of existence,
love, melancholy, and yearning.

But he feels somewhat weary as if he hadn't really had enough sleep, although a person should who stays at the *Imperial* and asks for a room with a window facing the *Musikverein*. Only someone who knows where he belongs or where he'd like to belong has special desires of this kind. In the last analysis, if he hadn't asked for this room, the manager at the reception desk would have had him escorted to this room anyway without a word, for that's why people came here, to the *Imperial*, and in such matters nothing happened here by chance. What made this hotel famous, unique, unequalled was the fact that sheer consideration and sensitivity prevented chance occurrences, but wherever you looked were concealed suggestions and, still more, concealed meanings.

Still in pajamas, he sampled his breakfast, which he had ordered from room service on account of the view; everything was there, nothing forgotten. Viennese pastry, good marmalade, Viennese coffee, and an egg, softboiled. Wool covers had been placed on the different pots and containers to keep the breakfast warm. The room was pleasantly heated, just right, so that you could get up, stand at the window in pajamas, and look out on the *Musikverein* and the St. Charles Church. He had slept well in spite of his slight weariness, or at least deeply, he had slept deeply, that often means something other than well, and he was at last sitting at breakfast, slightly weary as stated earlier, somewhat disheartened without cause, and felt Austrian, being alone in a warm room.

He was glad that his firm had paid for this trip, that this trip allowed him a good many hours of leisure, and he was comforted by the fact that this hotel shut out all kinds of things that would have bothered him here or anywhere else in the world and that leaped at him immediately when he stepped out on the *Ringstrasse,* not to mention other Viennese streets. This *Imperial* contained everything that he cared about and prevented everything unpleasant and unacceptable that conflicted with his arrivals everywhere else. Through the broad window the city of Vienna looked perfect, and his weariness, totally inappropriate to morning, was a small aftereffect of the preceding journey, not a factor in this sojourn. It became simply something imaginary that a cup of hot coffee would help him set aside in favor of a more playful mood, he hoped.

While he breakfasted, he tried to make sense of his absence from this Austria for so many years, and even if he couldn't make sense, at least to find an explanation. But all his thinking about it brought forth only excuses because it just wasn't so easy to explain a matter, regardless of what kind. Then no thoughts and no words sufficed, even if you had acquired hypocrisy with the birth certificate, if an empty smile was the only heirloom. It was surely a fact that he was an Austrian and that his passport would belong to the Republic of Austria all his life, although renewed at consulates, at one time here, another time there.

The trees that he could see from his window were bending with the wind, which was strong but childlike at the same time and which tossed in waves the senses of anyone walking in it. Because Vienna is usually windy, because the light is rarely clear but almost always hazy, because the stone angels blow trumpets that you either don't hear at all or hear everywhere, Austrians can live in Paris,

Rome, New York, or Bombay with no trouble because it doesn't make any difference, because they know how to live anywhere, where the lines are unclear, where the storm tears hearts loose from their fastenings, and where the light consists of longing. These Austrians can speak their language everywhere, their words are the true world language, the universal one, because nobody understands them, not even in Vienna. They open their mouths and say something that is meant differently than they express it, say something to be misunderstood or admired or laughed at, even ignored. That's possible everywhere, who knows, maybe even in other dimensions, of which the Austrians claim to know something, a little more than other people. He drew in the last drop of coffee, leaned back in his chair, and felt that he was smiling vainly without reason.

On the street he walked past girls so completely different from girls elsewhere he was almost convinced of having to love them all because of their rarity. He recalled the curious fact that he had never had a girl in Austria, and that presumably meant something, for he had lived in Austria for twenty years. When they came along on the *Ringstrasse* now, often in pairs, arm in arm, quite well dressed, he became interested for the first time in these young women and looked into their faces, which seemed slightly enervated and tired in spite of their beauty. This lassitude had nothing to do with their age, even the ones hardly past childhood showed it, and he sensed vaguely how quickly this exhaustion and visible sensibility could change into hysteria, or still more likely into melancholy.

The Viennese women were beautiful, beautiful enough to be desired, so that you would lean down to kiss them,

but then at the last moment, that second that precedes
a kiss, when the lips are almost touching, to recognize
quickly these fragile features and to avoid while blushing
the danger of a tenderness. He knew now why he had
never kissed an Austrian girl. It was the fear of fragility,
of the deadly restriction that would have originated from
it.

While he was walking along *Kärntnerstrasse,* former
comparisons occurred to him peculiar ones which, you
could say, were far-fetched, but not for him, the eternally
entangled one, for whom all relationships are direct, who
had learned to stammer the subjunctive with his first
words like all Austrian children. It was the nights of
New Year's, the midnight hours of his childhood when
the *Pummerin,* the biggest bell at St. Stephen's, rang out
through the countryside once again every year. Transmitted by radio, transmitted by the feeling of a transition
that is maintained for a few days like a state of intoxication, this bell rang, and the very thought that it hung in
Vienna, in St. Stephen's Cathedral, had made him shudder at that time. Now, walking along *Kärntnerstrasse,* he
came to this huge church but didn't go in and didn't look
upward to where the bell was known to be, which now
left him cold, almost bored him.

Much too much had turned cold since then while other
things, lesser things, almost glowed. The tomb of emperors, for example, radiated light, and the dead interred there
caused him pain. But the real emperors and kings that he
mourned were the boys leaning on the wooden railings
at the subway station. They were still living but had been
dead for a long time already, these boys had disintegrated

while they were playing in the highest spirits and conveyed gaping sadness when they burst out in jovial laughter. The emperors' vault and its district stretched across the playgrounds of the city of Vienna, and the councilwomen or ministers who presented these playgrounds to the public didn't even know that they were providing graves. The partly worn-through and somewhat speckled pants of these children stood close to the ostentatious bronze lids of the sarcophagi. He observed all of that with reverence, with meaningfulness, without irony.

The children's laughter bore its own seal of pain, which crept from the suburb into the heart chambers, into the main square of the city, the pain that didn't change from street to street. A pain without social classes, it was a neutral Austrian pain which is expressed in the fact that Viennese children stare at building sites somewhat longer as if they were questioning the thing to be built, that they lean somewhat more heavily on the wooden railings, more tired than they really are, these twelve-year-olds with their almost saintly names, with their perfectly beautiful faces and knowing eyes. They're named Florian or Sebastian and never achieve later the goal that's appropriate for such names. They roamed and roam through their city without pleasure, often stopped and stop and look around again and again as if they had missed something while walking, something available to take hold of. They look at things with great patience, their looking becomes almost staring at times. These boys behave differently than other children, and they finally see other images than they see in reality.

For them too the worst thing was still waiting, the

dispersal into many countries and the need to return to the Hotel *Imperial*, to this solid non-address. For them too the curse was still waiting, of no longer being able to speak their language, of hesitating before every syllable, of no longer bringing the dialect of childhood past their lips although they hungered for it so much. Florian and Sebastian too would enter a store and, like this visitor, out of fear of their own language ask for the desired object in English, an object that is unwanted as soon as it lies on the counter because of that mere hindrance.

Translated by Harvey I. Dunkle

The Death of a Bachelor

Arthur Schnitzler

SOMEONE HAD KNOCKED AT THE DOOR, quite gently, but the doctor awoke at once, turned on the light, and sat up in bed. He glanced at his wife who was sleeping quietly, picked up his dressing-gown, and went into the hall. He did not at once recognize the old woman who stood there, with the gray shawl over her head.

"The master is suddenly taken very bad," she said; "would the doctor be kind enough to come at once?"

ARTHUR SCHNITZLER (born in Vienna in 1862–died in Vienna in 1931) became a medical doctor like his father, but early on turned to literature, paralleling in his writings the discoveries being made by Sigmund Freud. Because his plays, prose writings, aphorisms, and especially the diaries that he kept for 45 years chronicle Viennese life and society more fully than the works of any other writer, Schnitzler is recognized today not only as the leading author of his generation, but also as one of the greatest Austrian writers. He is widely translated and continues to grow in popularity, not only because his themes of flirtation as a lifestyle, sex, love, interpersonal relationships, role playing, death, and the importance of chance in life are universal and timeless, but also because his brilliant, highly polished works continue to captivate readers. Stanley Kubrick made Schnitzler's *Traumnovelle* (*Dream Novel*) into the feature film *Eyes Wide Shut*.

Now he recognized the voice: it was the housekeeper of that old friend of his who had never married. The doctor's first thought was, "My friend is fifty-five years old, his heart has been out of order for years—it might well be something serious," and he said, "I'll come at once—will you wait for me?"

"Excuse me, doctor, but I have to hurry round to two other gentlemen," and she mentioned the names of the merchant and the author.

"But what is your business with them?"

"My master wants to see them again."

"See them again?"

"Yes, sir."

"He is sending for his friends," thought the doctor, "because he feels very near to death," . . . and he asked, "Is anyone with your master?"

"Of course," the old woman answered. "Johann is with him all the time." And she departed.

The doctor went back into his bedroom, and while he was dressing quickly and as noiselessly as possible, a feeling of bitterness came over him. It was not so much grief at the possibility of losing a good old friend, but the painful consciousness that they were all so far on in years, though not so long ago they had been young.

The doctor drove in an open carriage through the soft, heavy air of that spring night, to the neighboring suburb where his friend lived. He looked up at the bedroom window which stood wide open, and whence the pale lamplight glimmered into the night.

The doctor went up the stairs, the servant opened the door, greeted him gravely, and dropped his left arm in a gesture of grief.

"What?" asked the doctor, catching his breath. "Am I too late?"

"Yes, sir," answered the servant, "my master died a quarter of an hour ago."

The doctor heaved a deep sigh and went into the room. There lay his dead friend, with thin, bluish, half-open lips, his arms outstretched over the white coverlet; his meagre beard was in disorder, and a few gray wisps of hair had strayed over his pale damp forehead. The silk-shaded electric lamp that stood on the night table cast a reddish shadow over the pillows. The doctor looked at the dead man. "When was he last in our house?" he thought to himself. "I remember it was snowing that evening. It must have been last winter." They had not seen much of each other latterly.

From without came the sound of horses' hoofs pawing the road. The doctor turned away from the dead man and looked across at the slender branches of the trees swaying in the night air.

The servant came in and the doctor then enquired how it had all happened.

The servant told a familiar story of a sudden attack of vomiting and breathlessness. Then his master had leapt out of bed, paced up and down the room, rushed to his writing table, tottered back to bed again, where he lay racked with thirst and groaning and after one last effort to raise himself he had sunk back upon the pillows. The doctor nodded and laid his hand on the dead man's forehead.

A carriage drew up. The doctor went over to the window. He saw the merchant get out and glance enquiringly up at the house. Unconsciously the doctor let his hand

fall just as the servant had done who opened the door to
him. The merchant threw back his head as if refusing to
believe it, and the doctor shrugged his shoulders, left the
window, and sat down, in sudden weariness, on a chair at
the feet of the dead man. The merchant came in wearing
a yellow overcoat unbuttoned, put his hat on a small table
near the door, and shook the doctor by the hand. "How
dreadful!" he said; "how did it happen?" And he stared
dubiously at the dead man.

The doctor told him what he knew, and added: "Even
if I had been able to come at once, I could have done
nothing."

"Fancy," said the merchant, "it is exactly a week today
since I last spoke to him at the theater. I wanted to have
supper with him afterward, but he had one of his secret
appointments."

"What, still?" said the doctor, with a gloomy smile.

Outside another carriage stopped. The merchant went
to the window. When he saw the author getting out,
he drew back, not wanting to announce the sad news
by his expression. The doctor had taken a cigarette out
of his case and was twisting it about in an embarrassed
sort of way. "It's a habit I've had since my hospital days,"
he remarked apologetically. "When I left a sickroom at
night, the first thing I always did was to light a cigarette,
whether I had been to give an injection of morphia or to
certify a death."

"Do you know," said the merchant, "how long it is
since I saw a corpse? Fourteen years—not since my father
lay in his coffin."

"But—your wife?"

"I saw my wife in her last moments, but—not afterward."

The author appeared, shook hands with the other two, and glanced doubtfully at the bed. Then he walked resolutely up to it and looked earnestly at the dead man, yet not without a contemptuous twitch of the lips. "So it was he," he said to himself. For he had played with the question which of his more intimate friends was to be the first to take the last journey.

The housekeeper came in. With tears in her eyes she sank down by the bed, sobbed, and wrung her hands. The author laid his hand gently and soothingly on her shoulder.

The merchant and the doctor stood at the window, and the dank air of the spring night played upon their foreheads.

"It is really very odd," began the merchant, "that he has sent for all of us. Did he want to see us all gathered round his deathbed? Had he something important to say to us?"

"As far as I'm concerned," said the doctor, with a sad smile, "it would not be odd, as I am a doctor. And you," he said, turning to the merchant, "you were at times his business adviser. So perhaps it was a matter of some last instructions that he wanted to give you personally."

"That is possible," said the merchant.

The housekeeper had left the room, and the friends could hear her talking to the other servant in the hall. The author was still standing by the bed carrying on a silent dialogue with the dead man.

"I think," whispered the merchant to the doctor, "that

latterly he saw more of our friend. Perhaps he can throw some light on the question."

The author stood motionless, gazing steadily into the closed eyes of the dead man. His hands, which held his broad-brimmed gray hat, were crossed behind his back. The two others began to grow impatient, and the merchant went up to him and cleared his throat.

"Three days ago," observed the author, "I went for a two-hours' walk with him among the hills and vineyards. Would you like to know what he talked about? A trip to Sweden, that he had planned for the summer, a new Rembrandt portfolio just published by Watson's in London, and last of all about Santos Dumont. He went into all sorts of mathematical and scientific details about a dirigible airship, which, to be frank with you, I did not entirely grasp. He certainly was not thinking about death. It must indeed be true that at a certain age people again stop thinking about it."

The doctor had gone into the adjoining room. Here he might certainly venture to light his cigarette. The sight of white ashes in the bronze tray on the writing table struck him as strange and almost uncanny. He wondered why he was still there at all, as he sat down on the chair by the writing table. He had the right to go as soon as he liked, since he had obviously been sent for as a doctor. For their friendship had nearly come to an end. "At my time of life," he went on, pursuing his reflection, "it is quite impossible for a man like me to keep friends with someone who has no profession and never has had one. What would he have taken up if he had not been rich? He would probably have turned to literature: he was very clever." And he remembered many malicious but pointed remarks the dead man had made, more especially about the works of their common friend, the author.

The author and the merchant came in. The author assumed an expression of disapproval when he saw the doctor sitting at the deserted writing table with a cigarette in his hand, which was, however, still unlit, and he closed the door behind him. Here, however, they were to some extent in another world.

"Have you any sort of idea? . . ." asked the merchant.

"About what?" asked the author absentmindedly.

"What made him send for us, and just us?"

The author thought it unnecessary to look for any special reason. "Our friend," he explained, "felt death was upon him, and if he had lived a rather solitary life, at least latterly, at such an hour people who are by nature socially inclined probably feel the need of seeing their friends about them."

"He had a mistress, though," remarked the merchant.

"Oh, a mistress," repeated the author, and contemptuously raised his eyebrows.

At this moment the doctor noticed that the middle drawer of the writing table was half open.

"I wonder if his will is here?" he said.

"That's no concern of ours," observed the merchant, "at least at this moment. And in any case there is a married sister living in London."

The servant came in. He respectfully asked what arrangements he should make about having the body laid out, the funeral, and the mourning cards. He knew that a will was in the possession of his master's lawyer, but he was doubtful whether it contained instructions in these matters. The author found the room stuffy and close; he drew aside the heavy red curtains over one of the windows and threw open both casements, and a great waft of the dark blue spring night poured into the room. The doctor asked the servant whether he had any idea why the dead man had sent for him, because, if he remembered rightly, it was years since he had been summoned to that house in his capacity as doctor. The servant, who obviously expected the question, pulled a swollen-looking wallet from his jacket pocket, took out a sheet of paper, and explained that seven years ago his master had written down the names of the friends whom he wanted sent for when he was dying. So that, even if the dead man had been unconscious at the time, he would have ventured to send for the gentlemen on his own responsibility.

The doctor took the sheet of paper from the servant's hand and found five names written on it: in addition to those present was the name of a friend who had died two years ago, and another that he did not know. The servant explained that the latter was a manufacturer whose house the dead man used to visit nine or ten years ago, and whose address had been lost and forgotten. The three looked at each other with uneasy curiosity. "What does that mean?" asked the merchant. "Did he intend to make a speech in his last hours?"

"A funeral oration on himself, no doubt," added the author.

The doctor had turned his eyes on the open drawer of the writing table, and suddenly these words, in large Roman letters, stared at him from the cover of an envelope: "To my friends."

"Hullo!" he cried, took the envelope, held it up, and showed it to the others. "This is for us." He turned to the servant and, with a movement of the head, indicated that he was not wanted. The servant went.

"For us?" said the author, with wide-open eyes.

"There can be no doubt," said the doctor, "that we are justified in opening this."

"It's our duty," said the merchant, and buttoned up his overcoat.

The doctor had taken a paper knife from a glass tray, opened the envelope, laid the letter down, and put on his eyeglasses. The author took advantage of the brief interval to pick up the letter and unfold it. "As it is for all of us," he remarked casually, and bent over the writing table so that the light from the shaded lamp should fall on the paper. Near him stood the merchant. The author remained seated.

"You might read it aloud," said the merchant, and the author began.

"'To my friends,'"—he stopped with a smile—"yes, it's written here also," and he went on reading in a tone of admirable detachment. "'About a quarter of an hour ago I breathed my last. You are assembled at my deathbed, and you are preparing to read this letter together—if it still exists in the hour of my death, I ought to add. For it might so happen that I should come to a better frame of mind . . .'"

"What?" asked the doctor.

"'A better frame of mind,'" repeated the author, and continued: "'and decide to destroy this letter, for it can do not the slightest good to me, and, at the very least, may cause you some unpleasant hours, even if it does not absolutely poison the life of one or other of you.'"

"Poison our lives?" repeated the doctor, in a wondering tone, as he polished his eyeglasses.

"Quicker," said the merchant in a husky voice.

The author continued. "'And I ask myself what kind of evil humor it is that sends me to the writing table today and induces me to write down words whose effect I shall never be able to read upon your faces. And even if I could the pleasure I should get would be too trifling to serve as an excuse for the incredible act I am now about to commit with feelings of the heartiest satisfaction.'"

"Ha!" cried the doctor in a voice he did not recognize as his own. The author threw a glance of irritation at him, and read on, quicker and with less expression than before. "'Yes, it is an evil humor, and nothing else, for I have really nothing whatever against any of you. I like you all very well in my own way, just as you like me in your way. I never despised you, and if I often laughed at you, I never mocked you. No, not once—and least of all in those hours of which you are so soon to call to mind such vivid and such painful images. Why, then, this evil humor? Perhaps it arose from a deep and not essentially ignoble desire not to leave the world with so many lies upon my soul. I might imagine so, if I had even once had the slightest notion of what men call remorse.'"

"Oh, get on to the end of it," said the doctor in a new and abrupt tone.

The merchant, without more ado, took the letter from the author, who felt a sort of paralysis creeping over his fingers, glanced down it quickly and read the words: "'It was fate, my dear friends, and I could not alter it. I have had the wives of all of you: yes, every one.'"

The merchant stopped suddenly and turned back to the first sheet.

"The letter was written nine years ago," said the merchant.

"Go on," said the author sharply.

And the merchant proceeded. "'Of course the circumstances were different in each case. With one of them I lived almost as though we had been married, for many months. The second was more or less what the world is accustomed to call a mad adventure. With the third, the affair went so far that I wanted us to kill ourselves together. The fourth I threw downstairs because she betrayed me with another. And the last was my mistress on one occasion only. Do you all breathe again—my good friends? You should not. It was perhaps the loveliest hour of my life . . . and hers. Well, my friends, I have nothing more to tell you. Now I am going to fold up this letter, put it away in my writing desk—and there may it lie until my humor changes and I destroy it, or until it is given into your hands in that hour when I lie upon my deathbed. Farewell.'"

The doctor took the letter from the merchant's hands and read it with apparent care from the beginning to the end. Then he looked up at the merchant who stood by with folded arms and gazed down at him with something like derision.

"Although your wife died last year," said the doctor calmly, "it is none the less true."

The author paced up and down the room, jerked his head convulsively from side to side a few times, and suddenly hissed out through his clenched teeth, "the swine," and then stared in front of him as though looking for something that had dissolved into air. He was trying to recall the image of the youthful creature that he had once held in his arms as wife. Other women's faces appeared, often recalled but long since, he had thought, forgotten, but he could not bring before his mind the one he wanted. For his wife's body was withered and held no attraction for him, and it was so long since she had been his beloved. But she had become something other than that to him, something more and something nobler: a friend and a comrade; full of pride at his successes, full of sympathy with his disappointments, full of insight into his deepest nature. It seemed to him not impossible that the dead man had, in his wickedness, secretly envied him his comrade and tried to take her away. For all those others—what had they really meant to him? He called to mind certain adventures, some of old days and some more recent; there had been enough and to spare of them in his varied literary life, and his wife had smiled or wept over them as they went their course. Where was all this now? As faded as that far-off hour when his wife had flung herself into the arms of a man of no account, without reflection, perhaps without thought: almost as extinct as the recollection of that same hour in the dead skull that lay within on that pitifully crumpled pillow. But perhaps this last will and testament was a bundle of lies—the last revenge of a poor commonplace fellow who knew himself condemned to eternal oblivion, upon a distinguished man over whose works death has been given no power. This was not at all improbable. But even if it were true—it was a petty revenge and unsuccessful in either case.

The doctor stared at the sheet of paper that lay before him, and thought of his gentle, ever kindly wife, now growing old, who lay asleep at home. He thought also of his three children: of his eldest who was now doing his one year's military service, of his tall daughter, who was engaged to a lawyer, and of the youngest, who was so graceful and charming that a famous artist, who had lately met her at a ball, had asked if he might paint her. He thought of his comfortable home, and all this that surged up at him from the dead man's letter seemed to him not so much untrue as, in some mysterious way, almost sublimely insignificant. He scarcely felt that at this moment he had experienced anything new. A strange epoch in his existence came into his mind, fourteen or fifteen years before, when he had met with certain troubles over his profession, and, worn out and nearly crazy, had planned to leave the city, his wife and family. At the same time he had entered upon a kind of wild, reckless existence, in which a strange hysterical woman had played a part, who had subsequently committed suicide over another lover. How his life had gradually returned to its original course he could not now remember in the least. But it must have been in those bad times, which had passed away as they had come, like an illness, that his wife had betrayed him. Yes, it must so have happened, and it was clear to him that he had really always known it. Was she not once on the point of confessing it? Had she not given him hints? Thirteen or fourteen years ago. . . . When could it have been . . . ? Wasn't it one summer on a holiday trip—late in the evening on the terrace of some hotel? In vain he tried to recall those vanished words.

The merchant stood at the window and stared into the

soft pale night. He was determined he would remember his dead wife. But however much he searched his inmost consciousness, at first he could only see himself in the light of a gray morning, standing in black clothes outside a curtained doorway, receiving and returning sympathetic handshakes, with a stale reek of carbolic and flowers in his nostrils. Slowly he succeeded in recalling to his mind the image of his dead wife. And yet at first it was but the image of an image for he could only see the large portrait in a gilt frame that hung over the piano in the drawing room at home and displayed a haughty-looking lady of thirty in a ball dress. Then at last she herself appeared as a young girl, who, nearly twenty years before, pale and trembling, had accepted his proposal of marriage. Then there arose before him the appearance of a woman in all her splendor, enthroned beside him in a theater-box, gazing at the stage, but inwardly far away. Then he remembered a passionate creature who welcomed him with unexpected warmth on his return from a long journey. Swiftly again his thoughts turned to a nervous tearful being, with greenish heavy eyes, who had poisoned his days with all manner of evil humors. Next he saw an alarmed, affectionate mother, in a light morning frock, watching by the bedside of a sick child who, none the less, died. Last of all, he saw a pale, outstretched creature in a room reeking of ether, her mouth so pitifully drawn down at the corners, and cold beads of sweat on her forehead, who had shaken his very soul with pity. He knew that all these pictures, and a hundred others, that flashed past his mind's eye with incredible speed, were of one and the same being who had been lowered into the grave two years ago, over whom he had wept, and after whose death he had felt freed from bondage. It seemed to him he must choose one out of all these pictures to reach some definite reaction; for at present he was tossed by shame and anger, groping in the void. He stood there irresolute, and gazed across at the houses in their gardens, shimmering faintly red and yellow in the moonlight and looking like pale painted walls with only air behind them.

"Goodnight," said the doctor and got up.

The merchant turned toward him and said: "There's nothing more for me to do here either."

The author had picked up the letter, stuffed it unobtrusively into his coat pocket, and opened the door into the adjoining room. Slowly he walked up to the deathbed, and the others watched him looking down silently at the corpse, his hands behind his back. Then they turned away.

In the hall the merchant said to the servant: "As regards the funeral, it is possible that the will in possession of the lawyers may contain some further instructions."

"And don't forget," pursued the doctor, "to telegraph to your master's sister in London."

"To be sure, sir," replied the servant, as he opened the front door.

The author overtook them on the doorstep. "I can take you both with me," said the doctor, whose carriage was waiting.

"Thank you, no," said the merchant. "I shall walk."

He shook hands with both of them and walked down the road toward the city, glad to feel the soft night air upon his face.

The author got into the carriage with the doctor. The

birds were beginning to sing in the garden. The carriage drove past the merchant, and the three men raised their hats, ironically polite, each with an identical expression on his face. "Shall we soon see another play of yours?" the doctor asked the author in his usual voice.

The latter launched into an account of the extraordinary difficulties involved in the production of his latest drama which, he had to confess, contained the most sweeping attacks on everything generally held to be sacred. The doctor nodded and did not listen. Nor did the author, for the familiar sentences fell from his lips as though he had learned them by heart.

Both men got out at the doctor's house, and the carriage drove away.

The doctor rang. They both stood and said nothing. As the footsteps of the porter approached, the author said, "Goodnight, my dear doctor"; and he added slowly, with a twitch of his nostrils, "I shan't mention this to my wife, you know."

The doctor threw a sidelong glance at him and smiled his charming smile.

The door opened, they shook each other by the hand, the doctor disappeared into the passage, and the door slammed. The author went.

He felt in his breast pocket. Yes, the letter was there. His wife would find it sealed and secure among his papers. And with that strange power of imagination that was peculiarly his own, he could already hear her whispering over his grave, "Oh, how splendid of you . . . how noble!"

Translated by Erich Sutton

Beware of Pity

Stefan Zweig

OUR DECISIONS are to a much greater extent dependent on our desire to conform to the standards of our class and environment than we are inclined to admit. A considerable proportion of our reasoning is merely an automatic function, so to speak, of influences and impressions which have become part of us, and anyone who has been brought up from childhood in the stern school of military discipline is particularly apt to succumb to the hypnotic and

STEFAN ZWEIG (born in Vienna in 1881–died in Brazil in 1942) embraced the free lifestyle of the upper classes in dream world Vienna and embodied it completely to the end of his life. Influenced by Freud, he wrote novels and short narratives that delve into the psyches of characters facing a major crisis in their lives. As a pacifist, one of his favorite themes was the victor in defeat. He was the most widely translated of all German-speaking authors. To escape the Nazis, Zweig moved to England in 1934, then to the USA in 1940, and finally to Petropolis, Brazil. Eventually he wrote his autobiography, *The World of Yesterday*, which is truly the biography of Vienna and one of the most perceptive accounts about the city that he never ceased to love. When he realized that his Viennese world that shaped his life would never return, he chose to die by his own hand as a victor in defeat rather than face the dreary future he envisioned.

compulsive force exercised by an order or word of command; a force which is logically entirely incomprehensible and which irresistibly undermines his will. In the strait-jacket of a uniform, an officer will carry out his instructions, even though fully aware of their absurdity, like a sleepwalker, unresistingly and almost unconsciously.

I too, who, out of a lifetime of twenty-five years, had spent the really formative fifteen years first at a military academy and then in the army, ceased, from the moment I heard the Colonel's order, to think or to act independently. I no longer reflected. I simply obeyed. My brain only registered one thing—that I had to report, ready to march, at half past five, and by that time to make all my preparations without fail. Waking my batman, I informed him briefly that we had received urgent orders to leave for Czaslau in the morning, and helped him to pack up all my belongings. With some difficulty we managed to be ready in time, and on the stroke of half past five I was duly standing in the Colonel's room, waiting to receive the relevant official documents. In accordance with his orders, I left the barracks without being observed.

This hypnotic paralysis of the will, it is true, only lasted as long as I was still within the four walls of the barracks and I had not completely carried out my instructions. With the first jolt of the train, I threw off the stupor that had come over me, and started up like a man who, after having been hurled to the ground by a violent explosion, staggers to his feet and finds to his surprise that he is unhurt.

My first shock of surprise was to find that I was still alive; my second that I was sitting in a moving train, snatched out of my ordinary daily existence. And no sooner had I begun to remember the events of the night before than everything rushed at feverish speed through my mind. I had been about to make an end of things, and someone had knocked the revolver out of my hand. The Colonel had said he would put everything right. But only, as I realized to my consternation, in so far as the regiment and my so-called reputation as an officer were concerned. At this very moment, perhaps, my fellow officers would be standing before him, and it went without saying that they would all swear on their honor not to breathe a word about the incident. But no order could affect their inward thoughts, they would all be bound to realize that I had slunk off like a coward. The apothecary would, no doubt, let himself be talked round at first—but what of Edith, Kekesfalva and the others? Who was going to let them know, to explain the whole thing to them? Seven o'clock: she would just be waking up, and her first thought would be of me. Perhaps she was already on the terrace—ah, that terrace, why did I always shudder every time I thought of the balustrade?—gazing out through her binoculars at the parade ground, watching our regiment trotting along, not knowing, not suspecting, that someone was missing. But in the afternoon she would begin to wait, and I should not come, and no one would have told her anything. I had not written her a line. She would telephone, would be informed that I had been transferred, and she would not understand, would not take it in. Or more terrible still: she *would* understand, understand straight away, and then . . . Suddenly I could see Condor's eyes gazing out menacingly from behind his gleaming pince-nez. Once more I could hear him shouting at me: "It would be a crime, a murder!" And immediately another picture was superimposed upon the first; a picture of Edith as she had levered herself up out of her chaise longue and hurled herself against the balustrade—suicide, the abyss, mirrored in her eyes.

I must do something, do something at once! I must send a wire to her from the station, send her some message. I must at all costs prevent her doing something rash, irrevocable, in her despair. No, it was I who must not do anything rash, anything irrevocable, Condor had said, and if anything dreadful happened I was to let him know at once. I had promised him faithfully, and my word was my bond. Thank God, I should have two hours in Vienna to put this right, for my train did not leave until midday. Perhaps I should find Condor at home. I *must* see him.

On arrival I handed over all my luggage to my batman, telling him to go straight to the North-West Station and to wait for me there. Then I rushed off in a cab to Condor and kept praying (I am not as a rule religious): "Oh God, let him be in, let him be at home! He's the only person I can explain things to, the only one who can understand, who can help."

But the maid came shuffling toward me, a gaily colored handkerchief tied round her head. The *Herr Doktor* was not at home, she said. Could I wait for him? "'E no come till midday." Did she know where he was? "No, don' know. 'E go many places." Might I perhaps speak to the *Frau Doktor?* "I go ask," she said, shrugging her shoulders.

I waited. The same room, the same long wait as before,

and then, thank God, the same soft shuffling step in the next room!

The door was opened, timidly, uncertainly. As on the previous occasion, it was as though a puff of wind had blown it open, but this time the voice greeted me kindly and cordially.

"Oh, is it you, *Herr Leutnant?*"

"Yes," I said, bowing to the blind woman (foolish as ever).

"Oh, my husband will be sorry. I know he'll be terribly sorry not to have been at home. But I do hope you can wait. He'll be back in an hour at the latest."

"I'm so sorry, I'm afraid I can't wait. But . . . it's a very important matter . . . do you think I could get him on the telephone at the house of one of his patients?"

"No, I'm afraid that's impossible," she sighed. "I don't know where he is . . . and then, you see . . . the people he likes treating most are not on the telephone. But perhaps you could . . ."

She came nearer, and a shy expression flitted over her face. She wanted to say something, but I could see she felt embarrassed.

"I . . . I can tell," she managed to say at length, "I can tell that the matter must be very urgent . . . and if there were any possibility, I should . . . should, of course, tell you how to get hold of him. But . . . but . . . perhaps I could give him a message the moment he gets back . . . I suppose it's about that poor girl out there, to whom you've been so kind . . . If you like, I'll gladly undertake to do so . . ."

And now an absurd thing happened to me: I did not

venture to look this blind woman straight in the face. I
don't know why, but I had a feeling that she knew everything, had guessed everything. I felt ashamed, and could
only stammer out:

"It's very kind of you, *gnädige Frau*, but . . . I don't want
to trouble you. If you will allow me, I can leave a note for
him. But it's quite certain he'll be back before two, isn't
it? For the train goes just before two, and he must go out
there, I mean . . . it's absolutely essential, believe me, that
he should go out there. I'm really not exaggerating."

I could feel that she believed me implicitly. She came
nearer still, and I could see her involuntarily raising her
hand as though to comfort and reassure me.

"Of course I believe it, if you say so. And don't worry.
He'll do what he can."

"And may I write him a note?"

"Yes, do . . . Over there, please."

She walked ahead with the remarkable assurance of
one who knew every object in the room. A dozen times a
day her nimble fingers must have tidied up his desk, for
with the precision of one who could see she took three or
four sheets of paper out of the left-hand drawer and laid
them out quite straight on the blotter. "You'll find pen
and ink there," she said, again pointing to the exact spot.

I dashed off five pages. I entreated Condor to go out to
Kekesfalva at once, *at once*—I underlined the words three
times. I told him everything as briefly and frankly as possible. I had not held out, I had repudiated my engagement
in the presence of my fellow officers. He had correctly
surmised from the very beginning that my weakness had
been due to my fear of what other people would think,

my wretched fear of gossip. I did not conceal from him
the fact that I had intended to commit suicide and that
the Colonel had saved me against my will. But up to this
moment, I said, I had thought only of myself; only now
did I realize that I was bringing tragedy upon another, an
innocent, person. He must go out there *at once*—once more
I underlined the "at once"—he would, I knew, understand
how urgent it was, and tell them the truth, the whole
truth. He must not gloss over anything. He must not
represent me as better than I was, as innocent. If, despite
my weakness, she would forgive me, I should regard the
engagement as more sacred than ever. Only *now* had it
become really sacred to me, and, if she would allow me, I
would go with her to Switzerland straight away, I would
leave the service, I would stay with her no matter whether
she got well sooner or later or not at all. I would do everything possible to atone for my cowardice, my lies; the only
point of my life now was to prove to her that it was not
she whom I had betrayed, but only the others. He was to
tell her all this quite frankly, the whole truth, for only now
did I realize how much I was bound to her, far more than
to my comrades, to the service. She alone must judge me,
pardon me. The decision as to whether she could forgive
me was now in her hands, and would he please—it was
a matter of life and death—leave everything and go out
there by the midday train. He must be there by half past
four without fail, not a moment later, at the time when I
was usually expected. It was my last request to him. This
was the last time I should ever ask him to help me, and
he must go out there at once—four times I underlined the
scrawled "at once"—or all would be lost.

It was not until I put down my pen that I felt that I had made an honest decision for the first time. It was only while writing that I had realized what was the right thing to do. For the first time I felt grateful to the Colonel for saving me. I knew that from now on I was bound for life to one person alone, to the woman who loved me.

Not until this moment did I realize that the blind woman had been standing motionless at my side. A feeling, an absurd feeling, came over me that she had read every word of my letter and knew everything about me.

"Please forgive my rudeness," I said, springing to my feet, "I had entirely forgotten . . . but . . . but . . . it was so important to me to let your husband know at once . . ."

She smiled at me.

"Oh, it doesn't hurt me to stand for a little while. The other thing was all that mattered. My husband is sure to do whatever you ask him . . . I felt at once . . . you see, I know every tone in his voice . . . that he is fond of you, particularly fond . . . And don't torment yourself"—her voice grew warmer and warmer—"don't torment yourself, I beg you . . . everything's sure to be all right."

"God grant it!" I said, full of genuine hope, for had it not been said of the blind that they had second sight?

I bent down and kissed her hand. When I looked up, I could not understand how this woman with the gray hair, the harsh mouth, and that bitter look in her blind eyes had at first seemed ugly to me. For her countenance now shone with love and human sympathy. I felt as though those eyes that mirrored nothing but eternal darkness knew more of the reality of life than all those that gazed out, dear and radiant, upon the world.

Like a man cured of an illness I took my leave. The fact that at this moment I had pledged myself anew and for ever to another helpless outcast no longer seemed to me to entail a sacrifice. No, it was not the healthy, the confident, the proud, the joyous, the happy that one must love—they had no need of one's love! Arrogant and indifferent, they accepted love only as homage that was theirs to command, as their due. The devotion of another was to them a mere embellishment, an ornament for the hair, a bracelet on the arm, not the whole meaning and bliss of their lives. Only those with whom life had dealt harshly, the wretched, the slighted, the uncertain, the unlovely, the humiliated, could really be helped by love. He who devoted his life to them atoned to them for what life had taken from them. They alone knew how to love and be loved as one should love and be loved—gratefully and humbly.

My batman was waiting faithfully at the station. "Come along!" I smiled at him. All of a sudden I felt remarkably lighthearted, I knew with a feeling of relief such as I had never known before that I had done the right thing. I had saved myself, I had saved someone else. And I no longer regretted my senseless cowardice of the night before. On the contrary, I told myself, it was *better* so. It was better that it should have happened thus, that those who had faith in me should now know that I was no hero, no saint, no God who had graciously deigned to raise up a poor sick creature to sit beside Him in the clouds. If I now accepted her love, there was no longer any question of sacrifice. No, it was now for me to beg forgiveness, for her to grant it. It was better so.

Never before had I felt so sure of myself. Only once

did a fleeting shadow of fear touch me, and that was in
Lundenburg, when a fat man threw himself into the com-
partment, sank into a seat, and panted: "Thank the Lord
I've caught it! If it hadn't been six minutes late I should
have missed it."

Anxiety surged up within me for a moment. What if
Condor had not returned home at midday after all? Or if
he had come too late to catch the midday train? In that
case, all would have been in vain! She would wait and
wait. Once more there flashed through my mind that horrible scene on the terrace when she had clung to the balustrade and stared down into the depths below. Oh God,
she must be told in time how much I rued my treachery!
In good time, before she was plunged into despair, before
the worst happened! Perhaps it would be best if I sent her
a telegram at the next stop, just a few words to set her
mind at rest in case Condor should not have given her my
message.

At Brünn, the next station, I jumped out of the train
and rushed to the telegraph office on the platform. But
whatever was the matter? Outside the door was a surg-
ing throng, a black, clustering, excited mass of people, all
reading a notice. I had to elbow my way roughly through
to the little glass door in the post office. Quickly, quickly,
a telegraph form. What should I say? The great thing was
to be brief. "Edith von Kekesfalva, Kekesfalva. Thousand
greetings and best wishes. Called away on duty. Back
soon. Condor explaining everything. Writing on arrival.
Your devoted Anton."

I handed in the telegram. How slow the postmistress
was, what a lot of questions she asked: name and address

of sender, one formality after another! And my train was leaving in two minutes. Again I had to employ a good deal of force in order to push my way through the curious mob which was standing round the notice and had in the meantime swelled considerably. Whatever was the matter? I was just about to ask, when the whistle blew shrilly, and I just had time to leap into the carriage. Thank God, I had settled that, she could not be suspicious now, could not be uneasy! I was just beginning to realize how exhausted I was after those two nerve-wracking days, those two sleepless nights. And when, that evening, I arrived in Czaslau, I had to rally all my strength in order to stagger up to my hotel bedroom on the first floor, where I plunged into sleep as into an abyss.

I think I must have fallen asleep the moment my head touched the pillow—it was like sinking with numbed senses into a dark, deep flood, deep, deep down into depths of dissolution never otherwise reached. Only much later did I find myself dreaming a dream, of which I no longer remember the beginning. All that I can remember is that I was once more standing in a room, I think it was Condor's waiting room, and suddenly I could hear that dread wooden sound that for days had been hammering at my temples, the rhythmic sound of crutches, that terrible tap-tap, tap-tap. At first I could hear it in the distance as though it were coming from the street, then it came nearer—tap-tap, tap-tap—and then quite near, loud and insistent—tap-tap, tap-tap—and finally so horribly close to the door of my room that I started up out of my dream and awoke.

Wide-eyed, I stared into the darkness of the strange

room. But there it was again: tap-tap—the vigorous rapping of knuckles on hard wood. No, I was not dreaming now, someone one really was knocking on my door. I jumped out of bed and hastily opened the door. The night porter was standing there.

"The *Herr Leutnant* is wanted on the telephone."

I stared at him. I? Wanted on the telephone? Where . . . where was I, then? A strange room, a strange room . . . ah yes . . . I was in . . . Czaslau. But I didn't know a single soul here, so who could be ringing me up in the middle of the night? Absurd! It must be midnight at least. But "Please hurry, *Herr Leutnant*," insisted the porter. "It's a trunk call from Vienna. I couldn't quite catch the name."

In an instant I was wide awake. It could only be Condor. He must have some news for me.

"Go down quickly," I barked at the porter. "Tell them I'm coming in a moment."

The porter disappeared, and throwing my greatcoat as quickly as possible over my nightshirt, I hurried after him. The telephone was in a corner of the office on the ground floor; the porter was holding the receiver to his ear. I thrust him aside impatiently, although he was saying, "They've been cut off," and listened.

But I could hear nothing . . . nothing. Nothing but a distant buzzing and humming . . . bzz . . . bzz . . . brrr, a metallic droning as of mosquitoes' wings. "Hallo, hallo!" I shouted, and waited, waited. No reply. Nothing but that contemptuous, meaningless buzz. Was I shivering because I had nothing on over my shirt but my greatcoat, or was it sudden fear that was making my teeth chatter? Perhaps there had been a crisis. Or perhaps . . . I waited,

I listened, the hot rubber ring pressed close up against my ear. At last—krrx, krrx—the line was changed, and I could hear the voice of the operator:

"Did you get your call?"

"No."

"But you were through a moment ago. A call from Vienna! Just a moment, please."

Again that krrx, krrx. Then the line was changed again, and there was a squeaking, a clicking, a clucking, a gurgling, followed by a roaring and a whistling, which gradually died away into the faint humming and singing of the wires. Suddenly a voice, a harsh raucous bass:

"Headquarters, Prague, speaking. Is that the War Ministry?"

"No," I shouted in desperation. The voice rumbled on somewhat indistinctly and then faded out, was lost in the void. Once more that stupid singing and murmuring, and then once again a confused buzz of distant voices. Then I could hear the operator.

"Excuse me, I have been making inquiries. The line has been cleared. An urgent official call. I'll give you a ring the moment the subscriber calls again. Hang up your receiver, please."

I hung up the receiver, exhausted, disappointed, infuriated. There is nothing more exasperating than to have succeeded in capturing a voice from a distance and to be unable to hold it. My heart was pounding in my chest as though I had climbed up a mountain too quickly. Who could it have been? It could only have been Condor. But why was he telephoning me at half past twelve at night?

The porter came up to me politely. "The *Herr Leut-*

nant can perfectly well wait in his room. I'll rush up the moment the call comes through."

But I refused his offer. I mustn't miss the call a second time. I wasn't going to lose a single minute. I *must* know what had happened, for something—I could feel—had happened many kilometers away. It could only have been Condor or the Kekesfalvas. He was the only one who could have given them the address of my hotel. In any case it must have been something important, something urgent, or I should not have been fetched out of my bed at midnight. My tingling nerves told me that I was wanted, that I was needed. Someone wanted something of me. Someone had something extremely important to tell me, something that was a matter of life and death. No, I could not go away, I must remain at my post. I did not want to miss a minute.

And so I sat down on the hard wooden chair which the somewhat surprised porter brought for me, and waited, my bare legs hidden under my greatcoat, my gaze riveted on the instrument. I waited for a quarter of an hour, half an hour, shivering with anxiety and, I expect, with cold, again and again wiping away with my shirtsleeve the sweat that kept breaking out on my forehead. At last— rrr—a ring. I rushed to the instrument, snatched off the receiver. Now, now I should hear everything.

But I had made a stupid mistake, to which the porter immediately drew my attention. It was not the telephone that had rung, but the hotel bell, and a pair of late arrivals was admitted. A captain came bustling through the door with a girl, and they threw an astonished look in passing at the strange individual in the porter's lodge who,

bare-necked and barelegged, stared at them from out of
an officer's greatcoat.

And now I could bear it no longer. I turned the handle
and asked the operator, "Hasn't my call come through
yet?"

"Which call?"

"From Vienna . . . I think from Vienna . . . over half
an hour ago."

"I'll make inquiries. Just a moment."

That moment lasted an eternity. At last a ring. But the
operator merely said reassuringly:

"I'm still making inquiries. Just a moment. I'll ring you
again shortly."

Wait ! Wait another few minutes? Minutes? Minutes?
In the space of a second a human being can die, a fate
be decided, a world collapse! Why were they making me
wait, wait such a criminally long time? This was martyr-
dom, madness! It was already half past one by the clock.
I had been sitting about here, shuddering and shivering
and waiting, for an hour.

At last, at last, another ring. I strained all my senses to
listen, but the operator only said:

"The call has been cancelled."

Cancelled? What did that mean? Cancelled? "One
moment, Fräulein." But she had already rung off.

Cancelled? Why cancelled? Why did they ring me
up at half past twelve at night and then cancel the call?
Something must have happened of which I knew nothing
and which I yet must know. How awful, how horrible,
not to be able to penetrate time and distance! Should I
ring Condor up myself? No, not now in the middle of the

night. His wife would be frightened. Probably it was too late for him, and he had decided to ring up first thing in the morning.

Oh that night, I cannot describe it! Wild thoughts, confused images, chasing madly through my brain, and I myself dead-tired and yet wakeful, waiting and waiting with every nerve in my body, listening to every step on the stairs and in the corridor, to every ring and clatter in the street, to every movement and every sound, and at the same time reeling with weariness, washed out, worn out, and then, at last, sleep, far too deep, too long a sleep, timeless as death, abysmal as nothingness.

When I awoke, it was daylight. A glance at my watch: half past ten. My God, and I had been ordered by the Colonel to report immediately! Once again, before I had time to think of anything personal, the military part of my brain began to function automatically. I struggled into my uniform and rushed down the stairs. The porter tried to waylay me. No—everything else must wait till later. First I must report, as I had promised the Colonel on my word of honor.

My officer's sash properly adjusted, I entered the regimental offices. But there was no one there but a little red-haired noncommissioned officer, who stared up at me in dismay when he saw me.

"Please go down at once, *Herr Leutnant.* The Lieutenant-Colonel has given express orders that all the officers and men of the garrison must parade at eleven sharp. Please go down quickly."

I raced down the stairs. There they all were, the whole garrison, drawn up in the courtyard. I just had time to take my place next to the chaplain before the Divisional General appeared. He walked at a curiously slow and solemn pace, unfolded a document, and read out in a ringing voice:

A terrible crime has been committed which has filled Austria-Hungary and the whole civilized world with horror.—What crime? I thought in alarm. Involuntarily I began to tremble, as though I myself were the criminal— "The most perfidious murder . . ."—What murder?—"of the beloved Heir to the Throne, His Imperial Highness Archduke Franz Ferdinand, and Her Imperial Highness the Archduchess"—What? The heir to the throne had been murdered? When? Ah, of course—that was why there had been such a crowd round that notice in Brünn—that was it!—"has plunged our Imperial house into deep sorrow and mourning. But it is, above all, the Imperial Army which . . ."

I could scarcely hear the rest. I do not know why, but the word "crime" and the word "murder" had been like a stab at my heart. I could not have been more horrified had I myself been the murderer. A crime, a murder—those were the words Condor had used. All of a sudden I could no longer take in what this general in blue uniform with plumes and rows of decorations was babbling and shouting at us. All of a sudden I remembered last night's telephone call. Why had Condor not got in touch with me this morning? Had something happened, after all? Without reporting to the lieutenant colonel, I took advantage of the general confusion after the general's address to slip back quietly to the hotel. Perhaps a call had come for me in the meantime.

The porter handed me a telegram. It had arrived early

that morning, but I had rushed past him in such a hurry that he had been unable to give it to me. I tore it open. At first I could make nothing of it. No signature! A completely incomprehensible message! Then I understood: it was merely a communication from the post office to the effect that it had been impossible to deliver the telegram that I had handed in at 3:58 P.M. in Brünn the day before.

Impossible to deliver it? I stared at the words. Impossible to deliver a telegram to Edith von Kekesfalva? But everyone knew her in the little place. Now I could no longer bear the tension. I got a call put through to Dr Condor. "Urgent?" asked the porter. "Yes, urgent."

The call came through in twenty minutes and—melancholy miracle!—Condor was at home and himself answered the phone. In three minutes I heard everything—a trunk call doesn't give one time to mince matters. A devilish freak of fate had frustrated all my plans, and the unfortunate girl had not learned of my remorse, my sincere and honest resolve. All the steps taken by the Colonel to hush the matter up had proved in vain, for Ferencz and the others, instead of going straight home from the café, had gone on to the little bar, where, unfortunately, they had met the apothecary among a crowd of people, and Ferencz, the good-natured bungler, had, out of sheer affection for me, let fly at him. In the presence of everyone he had taken him thoroughly to task and accused him of having spread abominable lies about me. There had been a frightful scene, and the next day it had been all over the town, for the apothecary, feeling his honor called in question, had rushed straight off to the barracks next morning to compel me to bear him out in his story, and on being greeted with the highly suspicious news that I had disappeared, he had driven out to the Kekesfalvas'. Arrived there, he had burst in upon the old man in his office and stormed at him until the window panes rattled, saying that Kekesfalva had made a fool of him with his idiotic telephone message, and that he, as a respectable citizen, was not going to put up with insults from those impudent young cubs of officers. He knew why I had decamped in such a cowardly way; they couldn't humbug him into believing that it had merely been a joke; there was some thoroughgoing knavery on my part at the bottom of it all. Even if he had to go to the Ministry of War he would get the matter cleared up; he wasn't going to let himself be abused by a lot of snivelling youngsters in a public place.

It had only with difficulty been possible to calm him down and get him out of the house. In the midst of his consternation Kekesfalva had hoped for only one thing— that Edith should not hear a word of these wild surmises. But, as Fate would have it, the windows of the office had been open, and the apothecary's words had rung out with terrible distinctness across the courtyard and penetrated to the window of the salon, where she was sitting. She had no doubt decided to put her long-planned resolve into immediate effect, but she knew how to act a part; she had had her new clothes shown to her once more, she had laughed and joked with Ilona, had behaved charmingly to her father, had asked about a hundred and one details, and had inquired if everything was packed and ready. Secretly she had instructed Josef to ring up the barracks to inquire when I was coming back and whether I had not left a message. The fact that the orderly faithfully reported that I had been indefinitely transferred and had left no message for anyone had turned the scales. In her impetuosity she had refused to wait a day, an hour longer. I had disappointed her too profoundly, struck her too mortal a blow, for her to place any more faith in me, and my weakness had endowed her with fatal strength.

After lunch she had had herself taken up to the terrace. Inspired by some dim foreboding, Ilona had felt disquieted by her unexpected cheerfulness, and had not stirred from her side. At half past four—at the time when I usually turned up, and exactly a quarter of an hour before my telegram and Condor arrived—Edith had asked her faithful companion to fetch her a certain book, and, as Fate would have it, Ilona had complied with this seemingly innocent request. And the impatient girl, unable to tame her wild heart, had taken advantage of that one brief moment to put into effect her terrible resolve—just as she had told me she would on that very terrace, just as I had seen her put it into effect in my agonized dreams.

Condor had found her still alive. In some incomprehensible way her frail body had borne no external signs of serious injury, and she had been taken away unconscious in an ambulance to Vienna. Until late at night the doctors had hoped to be able to save her, and at eight o'clock, therefore, Condor had put through an urgent call to me from the sanatorium. But on that night of the 29th of June, the day on which the Archduke was murdered, all state departments were in a state of uproar, and the telephone lines were all engaged without interruption by the civil and military authorities. For four hours Condor had waited in vain to get through. Only when, just after midnight, the doctors had decided that there was no more hope, had he cancelled the call. Half an hour later she was dead.

Of the hundreds of thousands of men called to the war in those August days, few, I am certain, went off so nonchalantly, if not impatiently, to the front as I. Not that I was particularly war-minded. For me it was merely a way out, a means of escape. I fled into the war as a criminal flees into the darkness. The four weeks before war was declared I spent in a state of self-loathing, bewilderment and despair which I remember today with even more horror than the most ghastly moments at the front. For I was convinced that through my weakness, my pity, that pity which alternately advanced and receded, I had murdered a human being, the only human being who loved me passionately. I no longer ventured to go out into the streets; I reported sick, I hid away in my room. I wrote to Kekesfalva to express my sympathy (alas, it was really an acknowledgment of my guilt!); he did not reply. I overwhelmed Condor with explanations in self-justification; he did not reply. No word came from my fellow officers, nor from my father—probably because he was overburdened with work in his department during those critical weeks. I, however, saw in this unanimous silence universal condemnation. I became more and more a prey to the delusion that they had all condemned me, as I had condemned myself, that they all regarded me as a murderer, for that was how I regarded myself. While the whole Empire was quivering with excitement, while all over a distracted Europe the wires vibrated, were white-hot, with news of disaster,

while markets tottered, armies mobilized and the pru-
dent were already packing their trunks, I could think of
nothing but my cowardly treachery, my guilt. To be called
away from myself, therefore, meant release for me; the
war that drew into its vortex millions of innocent people
saved me, guilt-oppressed, from despair (not that I glorify
war on that account).

Melodramatic phrases revolt me. So I am not going to
say that I sought death. I shall only say that I did not fear
it, or at least feared it less than most people, for there were
moments when the thought of returning home, where I
should meet those who shared the knowledge of my guilt,
was more horrible to me than all the horrors of the front.
Where, moreover, was there for me to go? Who was there
who needed me, who was there who still loved me? For
whom, for what was I to go on living? In so far as bravery
is no more than not being afraid, I may safely and honestly claim to have been brave in the field, for even what
to the most valorous of my comrades seemed worse than
death, even the possibility of being crippled, of being
maimed, held no terrors for me. I should probably have
looked upon it as a punishment, as a just vengeance on
the part of Providence, to have myself been made a helpless cripple, the prey of every stranger's pity, because my
pity had been so cowardly, so weak. If, then, Death did
not cross my path, the fault did not lie with me; dozens
of times I went to meet him with the cold eye of indifference. Wherever there was any particularly difficult
task to perform, I would volunteer. Wherever there was
fierce fighting, wherever there was danger, I felt happy.
After being wounded for the first time I transferred to a

machine gun company and then later to the Air Force;
apparently I really did perform all sorts of daring feats
in our gimcrack machines. But whenever I read the word
"bravery" in a dispatch in connection with my name, I
had the feeling that I was a fraud. And whenever anyone
peered too closely at my medals, I turned quickly away.

When those four interminable years came to an end, I
discovered to my own astonishment that, despite everything, I was able to go on living in my former world. For
we who had returned from hell measured everything by
new standards. To have the death of a human being on
one's conscience no longer meant the same to a man who
had been to the front as to a man of the pre-war era. In the
vast bloodbath of the war my own private guilt had been
absorbed into the general guilt; for I was the same person,
it was the same eyes, the same hands, that had, after all,
set up the machine gun at Limanova which had mown
down the first wave of Russian infantry to advance on our
trenches, and I myself had afterward seen through my
field glasses the hideous eyes of those whom I had been
instrumental in killing, in wounding, and who, impaled
on barbed wire, groaned for hours until they died a pitiable
death. I had brought down an aeroplane on the outskirts
of Görz; three times it had turned a somersault in the
air until it crashed in the Alps and went up in a sheet of
flame, and then with our own hands we had searched the
charred and still gruesomely smoldering bodies for their
identity discs. Thousands upon thousands of those who
went to the war with me did the same, with rifle, bayonet,
hand grenade, machine gun and naked fist, hundreds of
thousands, millions of my generation, in France, in Russia

and Germany—of what moment, then, was one murder more, what mattered private, personal guilt in the midst of this thousandfold, cosmic destruction and wrecking of human life, the most appalling holocaust history had ever known?

And then—a further relief—in this world to which I returned there was no one left to bear witness against me. No one could reproach with past cowardice one so singled out for his special bravery. There was no one to call me a liar, a weakling. Kekesfalva had survived his daughter's death by only a few days. Ilona was living as the wife of an insignificant lawyer in a Jugoslav village. Colonel Buben-cic had shot himself on the Save. My fellow officers had either been killed in action or had long since forgotten the trivial episode—everything that had happened before the war had become as trivial, as valueless as the former Austrian currency. There was no one to accuse me, no one to judge me. I felt like a murderer who has buried the corpse of his victim in a wood: the snow begins to fall in thick, white, dense flakes; for months, he knows, this concealing coverlet will hide his crime, and afterward all trace of it will have vanished for ever. And so I plucked up courage and began to live again. Since no one reminded me of it, I myself forgot my guilt. For the heart is able to bury deep and well what it urgently desires to forget.

Only once did a reminder come to me from the other shore. I was sitting in the Vienna Opera House, in a cor-ner seat of the last row of the stalls, listening to Gluck's *Orphée*, the pure and restrained melancholy of which grips me more than any other music. The overture had just ended, and although the house lights did not go up for the brief interval, one or two stragglers were given an opportunity of finding their way in the dark to their seats. Two of these latecomers, a lady and a gentleman, hovered dimly at the end of my row.

"Excuse me please," the gentleman said, bowing politely to me. Without noticing or glancing at him, I stood up to allow them to pass. But instead of sitting down immediately in the empty seat next to me, he cautiously steered the lady ahead of him with gentle guiding hands; he showed her to her place, paved the way for her, as it were, thoughtfully pulled down the seat for her and helped her into it. This kind of attention was too unusual not to attract my notice. Oh, a blind woman, I thought, and involuntarily looked sympathetically in her direction. Then the somewhat portly gentleman sat down next to me, and with a pang I recognized him—it was Condor! The only man who knew everything, who knew the very depths of my guilt, was sitting so close to me that I could hear his breathing! The man whose pity had not, like mine, been murderous weakness but selfless, self-sacrificing strength; the only man who could judge me, the only man before whom I need feel ashamed! When, in the interval, the lights went up, he would be bound to recognize me.

I began to tremble, and hurriedly put my hand up to my face to be at least safe from discovery in the darkness. Not a bar more did I hear of the beloved music, so violently was my heart pounding. The proximity of this individual, the only man who really knew me, appalled me. As though I were sitting stark naked in the dark among all those well-dressed, respectable people, I shuddered at the thought of the moment when the blaze of light would reveal me. And so in the short space of time before the lights came on, and while the curtain was just falling on the first act, I hurriedly ducked my head and fled up the gangway—quickly enough, I think, for him not to see or recognize me. But ever since that moment I have realized afresh that no guilt is forgotten so long as the conscience still knows of it.

Translated by Phyllis and Trevor Blewitt

The Lovers

Elfriede Jelinek

ONE DAY brigitte decided that henceforth she wanted to be only a woman, completely a woman, for a type whose name was heinz.

she believes that from now on her weaknesses would be lovable and her strengths very concealed.

heinz, however, doesn't find anything lovable about brigitte, and her weaknesses he finds only disgusting.

ELFRIEDE JELINEK (born in Mürzzuschlag, Styria, in 1946) grew up in Vienna and studied art history and theater at the University of Vienna and music at the Vienna Conservatory. She is not only a versatile author of plays, novels, opera librettos and screenplays, but also a political activist. Her outspoken criticism of the government has led to her being labeled, like Thomas Bernhard, a *Nestbeschmutzer* (a bird that dirties its own nest). The media, which had concentrated on criticizing her, became adulatory enthusiasts the day after she was awarded the Nobel Prize for Literature in 2006. As a feminist, Jelinek describes the various ways women are exploited in such works as *Wir sind Lockvögel, Baby* (We Are Bait, Baby), *Die Liebhaberinnen* (*The Lovers*) and *Lust* (Lust). Her most popular work, *Die Klavierspielerin* (*The Piano Player*), which was made into a feature film, portrays a young concert pianist so controlled by her mother that she is driven to self-mutilation.

---

brigitte now also grooms herself for heinz, for when one is a woman, then one can no longer avoid this, then one also has to groom oneself. brigitte would like the future to reward her for this with a younger appearance. perhaps, however, brigitte has no future at all. her future depends entirely on heinz.

when one is young, then one always looks young, when one is older, then it is too late anyway. if one doesn't look younger then, the merciless judgment of society is: lack of cosmetic care during youth!

thus brigitte has done something that will be important in the future.

when one has no present, one must take precautions for the future.

brigitte sews bras. when one makes a short seam, one must make many of them; forty are, in any case, the absolute minimum in the specifications. if one makes a more complicated, longer seam, one must make correspondingly fewer of them. that is very human and just.

brigitte could get many workers, but she wants only heinz, who will become a businessman.

the material is nylon lace with a thin layer of foam rubber underneath. her factory has many marketing outlets in foreign countries and many seamstresses who come from foreign countries. many seamstresses leave for marriage, childbearing, or death.

brigitte hopes that she will one day leave for marriage and childbearing. brigitte hopes that heinz will take her out of here.

anything else would be her death, even if she remains alive.

for the present, brigitte still doesn't have anything except her name, in the course of the story, brigitte will get heinz's name. that is more important than money and possessions, that can procure money and possessions.

her real life, which is able to express itself when it is called upon, her real life is the life after work. for brigitte life and work are like day and night. thus we will talk more about her leisure time here.

in this special case, life is called heinz. the real life is not only called heinz, it also is heinz.

beyond heinz there is nothing. anything better than heinz is absolutely unreachable, unattainable for brigitte, anything worse than heinz, brigitte doesn't want. brigitte defends herself desperately with every means against the downward path, the decline that the loss of heinz represents.

but brigitte knows, too, that there is no upward path for her, there is only heinz or something worse than heinz or sewing bras to the end of her life. even now sewing bras without heinz means the end of life.

it is completely left to chance whether brigitte lives with heinz or departs from life and dies.

there are no rules for it. chance decides on brigitte's fate. not what she does and is matters, but heinz and what he does and is matters.

brigitte and heinz have no story. brigitte and heinz have only work. heinz is to become brigitte's story, he is to make her a life of her own, then he is to make her a child, whose future will in turn be determined by heinz and his profession.

the story of b. and h. is not something that becomes,

it is something that is suddenly there (like lightning) and is called love.

love comes from brigitte's side, she must persuade heinz that love also comes from his side. he must learn to recognize that for him, too, there can be no future without brigitte. naturally there is already a future for heinz, and, to be specific, as an electrician. he can have that, even without brigitte. one can lay electrical lines without b. even existing at all. indeed, even live! and one can go bowling without brigitte.

brigitte, however, has one task.

she must constantly make it clear to heinz that there is no future for him without her. that is a heavy strain. moreover, heinz must definitely be prevented from possibly seeing his future in somebody else. more about this later.

this is a stressful situation, but one promising success.

heinz wants to be and will become a small businessman of his own with his own small business. heinz will one day give orders, brigitte will receive orders. brigitte prefers to take orders from her own husband in his own business that will also in small part be her own business.

if only heinz doesn't one day meet a college student as, for example, susie! if only heinz doesn't, for heaven sakes, believe that somebody better than brigitte will ever exist, that such a person will also be better for him.

if heinz finds something better, he is supposed to let it go again. it would be best of all if he doesn't get to know it in the first place. that is also safer.

when brigitte sits at her sewing machine and does stretch stitching, feels the foam rubber and stiff lace under her fingers, the fashionably colored new enticing bra, then she has nightmares about somebody who does not yet exist, but whose path heinz could nevertheless cross in the form of something better.

brigitte doesn't get to relax even at work.

even at work she has to work. she is not supposed to think while working, nevertheless something in her is constantly thinking.

brigitte cannot make anything better out of her own life. anything better is supposed to come from heinz's life. heinz can free brigitte from her sewing machine, brigitte cannot accomplish that by herself.

but she has no assurance of that, because happiness is the result of chance and not a law or the logical consequence of actions.

brigitte wants to have her future made for her. she cannot create it herself.

the story of how the two became acquainted with one another is unimportant. the two are themselves unimportant. they are almost symptomatic of everything that is unimportant.

often male and female students—which is almost the same thing except for the sex—also meet one another. often one can tell exciting stories about such encounters.

such people sometimes even have a long earlier story.

although brigitte's early story is as unfavorable as one can imagine for the development of a future fortune, she has nevertheless met heinz in whose hands a fortune will some day develop.

brigitte is the illegitimate daughter of a mother who sews the same as brigitte, namely, bras and corsets.

heinz is the legitimate son of a truck driver and his wife who was allowed to stay home.

despite this gaping difference b. and h. have become acquainted.

in this special case, getting acquainted means wanting to escape or not wanting to let go and holding fast, respectively.

heinz has learned something that will one day open the whole world to him, namely, to be an electrician.

brigitte has never learned anything at all.

heinz is something, brigitte is nothing that others wouldn't be just as well without any effort. heinz is unique, and one also needs heinz often, for example, in case of damage to the wiring or if one needs some love. brigitte is interchangeable and unnecessary. heinz has a future, brigitte does not even have a present.

heinz is everything for brigitte, her work is nothing but a burdensome torment for brigitte. a human being who loves you is everything, a human being who loves you and in addition is somebody, that is the most brigitte can attain. her work is nothing because brigitte has it already, love is more because one has to find it first.

brigitte has already found: heinz.

heinz often asks himself what brigitte has to show.

heinz often plays with the idea of taking somebody else who has something to offer as, for example, cash or the property for a suitable business location.

brigitte has a body to offer.

besides brigitte's body many other bodies are thrown onto the market at the same time. the only positive thing that supports brigitte on this path is the cosmetic industry. and the textile industry. brigitte has breasts, thighs, legs, hips, and a cunt.

others have these things too, sometimes of even better quality.

brigitte has her youth which she also has to share with others, for example, with the factory and the noise there and the overcrowded bus. these things eat away at brigitte's youth.

brigitte is becoming older and older and less and less of a woman, her competition is becoming younger and younger and more and more of a woman.

brigitte says to heinz, "i need a person who will stand by me, who is there for me, and in return i will stand by him and will always be there for him."

heinz says he shits on that.

it's too bad that brigitte hates heinz so much.

today, for example, brigitte kneels on the cold floor before the toilet bowl in the little garden house of heinz and his parents.

this floor is colder than love, which is hot and is called heinz.

the truck-driving father is away, and brigitte is helping with the housework, which is the only way she can ingratiate herself, that is to say, she happily cleans the toilet with the shit-brush. five minutes ago she said she liked to do that. now she no longer likes doing it. she feels quite ill at the thought of all the shit that accumulates in the course of a week or so in a household of three people.

heinz will get for a wife, if not a secretary, a college student, a secretary, secretary or secretary. in any case he will get as his wife, a woman who is a real woman, thus knows how to handle the brush and its repulsive accompanying conditions.

brigitte doesn't help at home, that would mean putting capital and work into a small business undertaking that is condemned to failure, with losses from the beginning and without hope of success. hopeless. brigitte will do better to invest where something can come out of it. a whole new life.

since brigitte doesn't have many brains, the outcome is uncertain.

only managers, after all, have the brains to help them when they plan something. brigitte's fingers have been trained. nothing else. but these, with the arms attached could work for three if they had to. they have to. for heinz.

brigitte crawls into the ass of heinz's mother. there she also finds nothing but the same shit as in the toilet that she is just cleaning. but some day this will lie behind me, and then the future will lie ahead of me. no, when the shit is behind me, i will already be in the future. first i have to acquire a status which will enable me to be permitted to have a future at all. future is luxury. there is not all too much of it.

this little episode is intended to show nothing except that brigitte can work if she has to.

and she has to.

Translated by Donald G. Daviau

The Convent School

Barbara Frischmuth

I CAN'T SAY FOR SURE how and when it all began.
Maybe it was during the time when I was getting up day
after day at six o'clock, you know what that means: six
o'clock, one day after another, and I'm talking about a

BARBARA FRISCHMUTH (born in Altaussee, Styria in
1941) received her early education in a convent school, which
she made the subject of her first novel *Die Klosterschule* (*The
Convent School*), from which the excerpt here is taken. Under
the influence of Peter Handke and his concern for language,
she demonstrates in this critical work how the school used
language to inculcate the girls to assume a subordinate position in life as good wives and mothers in patriarchal Austria.
The book created a mild sensation and brought Frischmuth to
immediate critical and public attention. After training to be an
interpreter and translator at the universities of Graz, Vienna,
Erzerum, and Debrecen, she lived and studied in Istanbul. She
is considered an expert on Turkish affairs and is often called
upon to comment on multicultural matters in the newspaper.
She has written over forty books and has traveled widely, frequently to the United States, to give readings from her works
and lectures.

whole six weeks, if not longer. Sometimes I would lie
there awake from four o'clock on, just so I wouldn't sleep
in. It was almost summer by then and already light outside. Then I'd end up going to church without doing my
hair up or I'd get my blouse on backward. Then they'd
send me back out and tell me I had to make myself pre-
sentable. It isn't easy to explain how it all got started. I
had the feeling that something awful was going to happen to me. Mother Superior took me aside—it was after
vacation, not right away but a few weeks after the beginning of school—and she asked me if maybe something
had happened during vacation, if someone had "made
advances," and she said that I was, after all, a country
girl and when boys and girls get together for a swim, you
know, maybe at some out-of-the-way pond, perhaps a
secluded millpond, things *do* happen of course, and then
she asked whether I had remained "firm in my resolve."
She said I should feel free to confide in her, and if something actually had happened it was only a matter of my
"firm resolve" to see that something like that would never
happen again. And then she wanted to know whether
somebody might have touched me or whether I had let
somebody kiss me. She said that in my case "the worst"
didn't even cross her mind, though one must be prepared
for anything nowadays.

I said no, and that there was nothing the matter—what
on earth did she think might have happened?—and all
the time I was talking I looked her right in the eye till she
turned beet red.

And then there was that business with the acolyte. You
remember, not that tall one, the other one, who tripped

over the prayer stool and broke his leg. He even came to serve with his cast on.

After early Mass we pushed a letter to him through the rood screen—I mean I was the one who slipped it through, the others just came along so it wouldn't look so obvious. We'd drawn straws and decided it was me who was going to write him. And he passed the letter back to me as if it was something I had dropped accidentally. Imagine! Just went and handed it back to us through the screen. It didn't dawn on us until later that Sister Theodora was still in the chapel and could have been watching us from the choir—and of course we were late for breakfast too.

The last straw came a few days later when I fell asleep in bed lying beside Milla and you know very well what they can make out of that. They could've kicked us both out even though all we'd been doing was going over the homework for the next day, but try and tell *them* that! When we woke up the next morning and realized the trouble we were in, we still didn't know if the dorm Sister had seen us. But she's not one to say anything to you right afterward.

So I made a vow: if nothing comes of it, I'll go to early Mass every day for six weeks. Nothing happened, so I kept my vow, day after day. Even Mother Superior finally noticed, so she took me aside again and asked if I were doing penance for something really serious. She said I should feel free to confide in her. I told her no, it was nothing, really, just that my uncle had died suddenly and I wanted to say a novena for the remission of his sins. She patted me on the cheek and said there's a good girl, but I'll bet she didn't believe a word of it.

The funny thing is that I haven't had any visions lately. Not even when I kneel through the whole Mass. My arms and legs do go all shaky and the Host does seem to shimmer if I stare at the light long enough, but it's nothing like at May devotions last Spring. And my stomach rumbles during the Consecration, and once I even got cramps.

Milla thinks I should go see Crossbill and ask him why I don't have visions any more, but I'm not about to go—you know how skeptical the Church is about these things, and Crossbill said himself that you've got to be careful about things like that because nobody can tell if Satan mightn't be using it as a golden opportunity, and he said that the Church is always the last to accept this sort of thing "without first subjecting it to a most rigorous and thorough investigation."

For me this can only mean one of two things: either I was fooling myself back then, or I *have* fallen from Grace. And anyway, the Church would never accept my visions as authentic. So why bother to go see Crossbill?

And now for the first time in my life I'm getting really fed up with those countless prayers he'd be sure to prescribe "to strengthen me against Evil." My inner voice tells me that's a thing of the past anyhow, with or without Prayers Penitential and Prayers Supererogational. Or is this the Devil Himself talking out of my mouth?

What's more, I do have serious doubts. They say that's a good thing. The greater the doubt, the stronger the belief. And that puts us right back where we were before. I'm not trying to tell you that my faith is gone, the way yours is. There *is* probably something to it after all. They couldn't simply have made it all up, because you can't make something out of nothing, but I don't want to get into that because it won't get you anywhere.

It's that business with the "vows" that I now find so hard to take. It's as if somebody owed me something. As if I'd paid too much for too little. Or else the whole business *is* fishy—there was no point to it somehow, or maybe there *was* a point—but it really doesn't make any difference any more, or maybe it does, I just don't know what to think.

And that's why I am writing you back even though we're not supposed to answer you. I've found a way to smuggle it out without anyone noticing. One of the day-help will mail it, you know who I mean. I don't want to write a name down because they might get their hands on this letter.

I'm sleeping better now, still dreaming a lot but at least my dreams are pleasant. I haven't had to throw up for quite a while. It's a strange feeling, being here and yet not being here the way I used to be. Apart from that, it's all pretty much the way it usually is this time of year. We go around in short-sleeved blouses, and the dorm windows are left open at night.

In spite of all that's happened, you must be doing all right. Maybe I should've had more confidence in myself back then, the way you did. It all boils down to having enough courage to make a choice if you have one.

But for me there *is* no other choice. If I get thrown out of here, school is over and done with and I'm on my own. You're just lucky there's a school in your town you can go to.

Milla and I often talk about what it'll be like when

we don't *have* to be here anymore. Milla always says the world will be totally changed. But I tell her we're the ones who will change. We certainly won't come back to visit, no matter how much we intend to now. What's going on here won't be of any interest to us at all. And if by some fluke we do drop in, then it will turn out to be just when Sister Amy—our dear Sister Amy—is sure to be busy teaching and we won't have time to wait till she finishes her class. Mother Superior will tell us what angels we were, compared to the ones who've come since, and that we look so much worse than we did when we were their charges. And Sister Assunta will whisper in our ear that she'd never ever hear stories as good as the ones she overheard us tell, and that she still prays for us.

We'll probably even bring them something—except for Sister Theodora—but of course we know they'll put any flowers we bring in the chapel and Sister Amy gets a rash from chocolate and Mother Superior will sell hers to the girls on Sundays at her desk in the study hall. And they'll look like real people to us because what we do is none of their business anymore.

But, before that happens, they've got all the time in the world to shape us up—they're not about to spare the rod and spoil the child—and they'll cure us of any smart ideas about getting too big for our britches. Let every soul be subject unto the higher powers. For there is no power but of God: the powers that be are ordained of God. Whosoever therefore resisteth the power, resisteth the ordinance of God. And does not our Holy Catholic Faith reveal to us the meaning and purpose of life? For it is only within that Faith that Salvation lies, all that is necessary for our Salvation can be found within it etc. etc.

And now you say you don't believe anymore. I just wonder how you manage not to. Aren't you afraid of the Hereafter? And aren't you sorry sometimes? And what makes you so sure you're right? After all, Lourdes is a proven fact, Fatima too, and there's got to be something to it—it didn't just happen by itself. There's even a book called *The Bible as History*. And doesn't your conscience ever bother you? And if you really don't believe anymore, why don't you do whatever you want, I mean absolutely anything? Why don't you just pack up and go, why don't you take all your clothes off in the middle of the street, or just go ahead and grab whatever you want? You'll probably say you don't think that kind of thing would be any fun for you. But there must be *something* that's forbidden and at the same time fun for you. Why don't you do it then? Or *are* you doing it?

You've got to write me again. You know what address to use. What I want to know most is if you're doing what's fun for you, and if you aren't then why you aren't? I'd be doing it for sure, if I were free like you.

Translated by Gerald Chapple and James B. Lawson

Woodcutters

Thomas Bernhard

WHEREVER I TRAVEL I prefer to be alone, just as I prefer to be alone when I am out *walking*. Yet it had always been a great joy to know that at the end of the journey to Kilb I would find Joana in her parents' little one-story house. I always made these journeys in the spring or the fall, never in summer and never in winter. Country girls, as soon as they are capable of making plans, set their sights on Vienna, the big city, I thought as I sat in the wing chair,

---

THOMAS BERNHARD (born in Heerlen, Holland in 1931–died in Gmunden, Upper Austria in 1989) began by writing poetry but soon turned to novels and plays, all characterized by his gift for uniquely stylized language. His protagonists engage in lengthy monologues, repetitiously dispensing their quirky views of life and other people. He pilloried Austria frequently and unrelentingly, so much so that he became castigated by some critics as a *Nestbeschmutzer*. Ironically, the more Bernhard criticized the state, the more awards and honors he received. Many readers at home and abroad find delight in his seemingly pessimistic writings, relishing the humor of his exaggerations. All of his major works have been translated into English, and he has become a great favorite of American authors, who strive to emulate his form and style, if not his subject matter.

---

and that hasn't changed. Joana had to go to Vienna, as she
wanted at all costs to make a *career* for herself. She just
couldn't wait for the day when she would board the Vienna
train for good, so to speak. But Vienna brought her more
heartache than happiness, I thought, sitting in the wing
chair. Young people set off for the capital and come to
grief, in the truest sense of the word, in the very place
where they have placed all their hopes, thanks to the
appalling society they find there, as well as to their own
natures, which are generally no match for this cannibalis-
tic city. After all, Auersberger too had set his heart on
making a career in Vienna, yet he'd made no more of a
career there than Joana; all this time he's been chasing
after a career that has so far eluded him, I reflected in the
wing chair. He made life too easy for himself, I thought,
sitting in the wing chair, and so did Joana: when it comes
to making a career in the big city things don't just happen
by themselves, and in Vienna they're even less likely to
happen by themselves than they are elsewhere. The mistake they both made, I now reflected in the wing chair,
was to think that Vienna would come to their aid, that it
would grab them under the arms, so to speak, and stop
them from falling. But the city doesn't grab anyone under
the arms: on the contrary, it constantly seeks to fend off
the unfortunate people who repair to it in search of a
career, to destroy them and annihilate them. It destroyed
and annihilated not only Joana, but Auersberger too, who
once believed that in Vienna he would be able to develop
into an important composer, a composer of international
importance, though to tell the truth he was not only
unable to develop in Vienna—he was utterly ruined by the

city. The genius he brought with him from Styria, of which there were unmistakable signs some thirty years ago, I now reflected, soon wasted away in Vienna; first it suffered a body blow, and then it became stunted, like countless other geniuses before it, especially musical geniuses. In Vienna he inevitably succumbed to atrophy and dwindled into a so-called *successor of Webern*, and he has remained a *successor of Webern* ever since. And Joana dreamed all her life of making a career for herself as a ballerina at the Opera, and finally of becoming a famous actress at the Burgtheater, yet all her life she remained a dilettante both as a dancer and as an actress, a movement therapist, so to speak, giving private lessons in deportment. It's now twenty-five years, I thought, since I used to write playlets for her, which she would then perform for me during the afternoons and evenings we spent in her high-rise in the Simmeringer Hauptstrasse, and which we would record on tape for all time, as it were—dozens of pieces for two voices, in which she would try to prove how gifted she was and I would try to show off my literary and histrionic talents. These plays have been lost; they were quite devoid of literary merit, but for years they kept Joana and me alive, I now thought, sitting in the wing chair. For years I would set out, every two or three days, from my apartment in the Eighteenth District and catch the No. 71 tram out to the Simmeringer Hauptstrasse, call at Dittrich's liquor store opposite Joana's high-rise and buy three or four two-liter bottles of the cheapest white wine, then take the elevator to Joana's apartment on the eleventh floor. As we drank we would practice the *total theatrical art*, which comprises both acting and play writing, more or less relying on the wine to sustain us, until we were quite exhausted. When we were no longer capable of performing, we would play back the recordings we had made and get high on them until well into the night, in fact until morning came. My relationship with Joana, I reflected in the wing chair, played an important part in my own development. It was Joana who brought me back to the theater, which I had abandoned after passing out of the Academy. I'd left the Academy with my certificate, I now recalled, thinking as I went down the staircase that I was now through with theater studies and that I wanted nothing more to do with the theater for the rest of my life. I actually shunned the theater for years, until Auersberger introduced me to Joana. Then the moment I met her she suggested the idea of writing playlets for her—short dramatic sketches, in other words. She had the perfect voice. It was not *the way she looked* that fascinated me, but *the way she spoke*. And in fact it was my acquaintance with her, which eventually developed into a friendship, that quite simply brought me back into contact with art and things artistic, after I had been averse to them for so long. For me Joana, and everything about her, represented the theater. Besides, her husband painted, and this also fascinated me, right from the beginning, I recalled in the wing chair. Under the right circumstances she could probably have become one of the greatest artists, either as a dancer or as an actress, I thought as I sat in the wing chair, had she not met her artistic husband, Fritz, the painter turned tapestry artist, and had she not given in when she came up against the first serious obstacles to her ambition. On the other hand those of her fellow students from the Reinhardt

Seminar who actually went on to act at the Theater in the Josefstadt or the Burgtheater, although they are now famous, succeeded only in becoming rather ridiculous and basically futile theatrical figures, who appear in perhaps one Shakespeare play, one Nestroy play and one Grillparzer play a year and are assuredly a thousand times more stupid than Joana ever was. This evening's gathering, though planned as an *artistic dinner* in honor of the actor, is in fact only a requiem for Joana, I said to myself: the smell of that afternoon's funeral was suddenly present in the Gentzgasse, the smell of the cemetery at Kilb was here in the Auersbergers' apartment. This so-called *artistic dinner* is really a funeral feast, I thought, and at once it occurred to me that to my certain knowledge the actor we were waiting for was the only supper guest who had *not* known Joana. The date for this *artistic dinner* had already been agreed, first of all with the actor from the Burgtheater, before Joana killed herself; the Auersbergers had said more than once that it was intended as a belated celebration of the premiere of *The Wild Duck*, which had just opened at the Burgtheater. Joana's death had intervened in their dinner arrangements; they told the guests that it was a dinner in honor of the actor, but then intimated— though not in so many words—that it was in memory of Joana. The actor's convinced that this *artistic dinner* is being given for him, and that's enough to satisfy the Auersbergers, though of course they are giving it more for Joana, since it's taking place on the day of her funeral, I thought, sitting in the wing chair. At that moment I recalled that on the previous day I too had intended to read *The Wild Duck*, in order to be able to keep up with the actor, thinking that I needed only to open my bookcase and get out the text. But I was wrong: I had no copy of *The Wild Duck*, though I had been convinced that I had one. I'm bound to have a copy of the play, I had thought as I opened my bookcase. I've read it several times during the course of my life, I had thought, and I can even remember what the editions look like. But I really did not have a copy, and so, like Jeannie Billroth, I decided to buy myself one in town, but was unable to find one. However, sitting in the wing chair, I remembered that one of the characters in the play was called *Old Ekdal*, and that he had a son, *Young Ekdal*, who was a photographer. And I remembered that the first act took place at the home of a manufacturer called Werle. Ekdal has a studio in the attic, I reminded myself; gradually it all came back, and so I no longer had to exert my memory. Can this production of *The Wild Duck* be any good, I wondered, sitting in the wing chair, *if it's being put on by actors from the Burgtheater*? And again I thought of the *Iron Hand*, where I had taken the woman from the general store, who was dressed all in black, after arriving at Kilb. I entered the store only for a moment, to let her know that I had arrived. She immediately put on a black coat and accompanied me to the *Iron Hand*, the operations room, so to speak, for Joana's funeral. We both ordered a small goulash and waited for Joana's companion to arrive. He arrived at about half past eleven and joined us at our table. When people are dressed in black they appear unusually pale, and this companion of Joana's (the woman from the general store insisted on calling her *Elfriede*) was so pale that he looked as though he were about to vomit at any moment. He actually did feel like vomiting when he approached our table, as he had come straight from the mortuary chapel next to the church, where he said he had been shattered by what they had shown him: without any prior warning he had had to *endure the sight* of Joana's body in a plastic bag. It appeared that the mortician, who as usual was the local carpenter, had been given no precise instructions about how the deceased was to be buried and had simply put Joana's body in a plastic bag pending the arrival of her companion that morning—this being the cheapest way of dealing with it—and left it on a trestle support in the mortuary chapel. He told us that on seeing the plastic bag he had felt sick and instructed the sexton to cover the body in a shroud and put it in a beech coffin; these instructions had been carried out with his assistance. While we all ate our goulash he told us that he simply could not describe what it had been like to pull Joana's body out of the plastic bag and cover it with a shroud—it had all been so *gruesome*. Finally he had chosen the most expensive coffin the carpenter had in stock. Having eaten half his goulash he went out into the corridor to wash his hands; when he returned I could see tears in his eyes. There were no relatives left, he said; they'd all *died on her* long ago, as he put it, and so all the funeral arrangements *fell to him*. He had expected that the woman from the general store would have seen to Joana's body and everything arising from her suicide, but at this she shook her head and said that she could not have left her shop even for an hour and had assumed that he had all the arrangements in hand. Be that as it may, Joana's companion ate his goulash so quickly that he had already finished it when I was only halfway through mine. He accidentally splashed some of the gravy on his white starched shirt—or rather on his white starched shirtfront, for I noticed that he was not wearing a shirt, only a shirtfront over a woolen undervest, I recalled in the wing chair. This starched shirtfront spotted with gravy more or less confirms my impression that Joana's companion was completely down and out, I thought as I sat in the wing chair. Having finished his goulash he waited impatiently for us to finish ours, but neither of us could eat any faster. In the end I left nearly half of mine, but the woman from the general store managed to force down the rest of hers. If there's nobody around to pay the expenses, said Joana's companion, they simply put the body in a plastic bag. And then he said that there had been a frightful *stench* in the mortuary chapel. Looking out of the window of the inn, I saw several cars go past with people I knew in them; they had clearly come to Kilb for the funeral and were making for the cemetery. What a good thing I've brought my English umbrella with me, I thought, when it began to rain. The street outside grew dark, and the inn parlor even darker. Jeannie Billroth, the writer, walked past with her retinue, all of them young people under twenty. It was actually *in the high-rise* that I last saw Joana, I now recalled saying to myself in the *Iron Hand*; her face was bloated and her legs swollen. She spoke in what anybody would have described as a *drunken voice*. Over the bed hung one of her husband's tapestries, thick with dust, a reminder of the fact that she had once been happy with this man. The apartment was full of dirty laundry and stank abominably. The tape recorder by the bed, where I could see she spent virtually the whole day, was out of order. On the floor were dozens of empty white wine bottles, some standing, some knocked over. I wanted to hear a particular tape we had made four or five years before this surprise visit of mine, a tape of a sketch in which I had played a king and Joana a princess, but the tape was nowhere to be found. Even if we had found it there would have been no point, as the tape recorder was broken. *Naturally you were a naked princess*, I said to Joana as she lay in bed. *And you were a naked king*, she replied. She tried to laugh, but could not. There was nothing touching about this last visit of mine, nothing sentimental, I thought, sitting in the wing chair—I found it simply nauseating. There were signs of a companion about the apartment—a pack of cigarettes here, an old tie there, a dirty sock, and so on. She told me several times that I had let her down. She could hardly sit up in bed; she tried several times, but each time she fell back. *You let me down, you let me down*, she kept on saying. For the last few years, she said, she had lived by selling off the tapestries her husband had left behind. She had not heard from Fritz. And she had not heard from the others either—she meant *the artistic crowd*—she had heard *nothing from any of them*. She asked me to go down to Dittrich's and get two two-liter bottles of white wine. *Go on!* she said, just as she always had, Go *on! Go on!* She ordered me down to the liquor store, and I obeyed, just as I had done twenty or twenty-five years before. When I got back I put the two bottles by the bed and took my leave. There would have been no point in having any further conversation with her, I told myself as I sat in the wing chair. At the time I thought she was finished, yet she went on living for several years, and that was what amazed me most. I can truthfully say that until I learned of her death I had assumed that she must have been dead for years. Not having seen her or heard from her for so many years, I had simply forgotten about her, I thought, sitting in the wing chair. The truth is that at times we are so close to certain people that we believe there is a lifelong bond between us, and then suddenly they vanish from our memory overnight, I thought as I sat in the wing chair. It's the way with actors, I told myself, sitting in the Auersbergers' wing chair, that they don't dine much before midnight, and those who keep company with actors have to pay for this dreadful habit of theirs. If we go to a restaurant with actors the soup is never served until half past eleven at the earliest, and the coffee stage isn't reached until about half past one. *The Wild Duck* is a relatively short play, I told myself, but then it takes at least half an hour to get from the Burgtheater to the Gentzgasse, and after the performance the actors have to take their curtain calls—and since *The Wild Duck* is such a great success, there'll have been fairly prolonged applause—so it'll be at least half an hour before the actors have taken off their makeup. So if the performance finished at ten thirty it'll take the actor, who after all is the person for whom this *artistic dinner* is being given, at least until twelve thirty to get to the Gentzgasse. The Auersbergers invited their guests for half past ten—that's monstrous, I told myself as I sat in the wing chair: they must have known that *The Wild Duck* went on till ten thirty and that consequently their Ekdal couldn't be in the Gentzgasse before half past twelve. If I'd thought carefully about when this *artistic dinner* was

actually going to start, I certainly wouldn't have come, I
thought. I go to the Graben to look for a tie, which naturally I don't find, I thought, and at the most inauspicious
moment I run into the Auersbergers. It's as though time
had stood still, I thought: all the guests at this *artistic dinner* are people who were their closest and most intimate
friends thirty years ago, back in the fifties. Clearly none of
these friends had ever severed their relations with the
Auersbergers; throughout the twenty or thirty years in
which I had had no contact with the Auersbergers, all
these people had kept up with them, as they say. I suddenly felt like a deserter, a traitor. It's as though I'd
betrayed the Auersbergers and everything I associate with
them, I thought, and the same thought must have occurred
to the Auersbergers and their guests too. But that did not
worry me—quite the contrary, for even now, sitting in
their wing chair in their apartment, I found the Auersbergers utterly repugnant, and their guests equally so;
indeed I hated all of them, because they were in every way
the exact *opposite* of myself. And now, as I tried to sit it out
in the Auersbergers' apartment, anesthetized by a few
glasses of champagne, I felt that my dislike of them had
in fact always amounted to hatred, hatred of everything to
do with them. We may be on terms of the most intimate
friendship with people and believe that our friendship
will last all our lives, and then one day we think we've
been let down by these people whom we've always
respected, admired, even loved more than all others, and
consequently we hate and despise them and want nothing
more to do with them, I thought as I sat in the wing chair;
not wanting to spend the rest of our lives pursuing them

with our hatred as we previously pursued them with our love and affection, we quite simply erase them from our memories. In fact I succeeded in evading the Auersbergers for more than two decades and avoiding any risk of meeting them, having devised a deliberate strategy for avoiding any further contact *with these monsters*, as I could not help calling them privately, and so the fact that I had evaded them for over twenty years was in no way fortuitous, I thought, sitting in the wing chair. Joana's suicide alone is to blame for the fact that, in spite of everything, I quite suddenly ran into them in the Graben. Their abrupt invitation to their dinner in honor of the *Wild Duck artist* and my equally abrupt acceptance were a classic illustration of the irrational way one reacts under stress. After all, even though I'd accepted the invitation, I didn't have to act upon it, especially as I've never been punctilious about keeping my promises to visit people, I thought. In fact during the whole of the interval between being invited to this *artistic dinner* and the dinner itself I had kept on wondering whether I would really go to it. At one moment I thought I would, at another I thought I wouldn't; now I told myself I'd go, now I told myself I wouldn't go. I'll go, I won't go — this word game went on in my head day after day, almost driving me insane, and even this evening, shortly before I finally set off for the Gentzgasse, I still wasn't sure whether I would go to the Gentzgasse. Only a few minutes before I finally decided to go I said to myself, Since you've just seen all over again, at the funeral in Kilb, that the Auersbergers are as repulsive as ever, you naturally *won't* go. The Auersbergers are repulsive people; it was they who betrayed you, not you who betrayed them, I

kept thinking as I tried to freshen up in the bathroom,
running ice-cold water over my wrists and at one stage
trying to cool my face by holding it under the tap. Over
the past twenty years they've run you down and deni-
grated you wherever they could, perverting the truth
about everything connected with you and taking every
opportunity to assassinate your character, I thought;
they've told stories about you that aren't true, they've
spread lies about you, vicious lies, more and more lies,
hundreds and thousands of lies in the last twenty years,
telling everybody that it was *you* who exploited *them* at
Maria Zaal, not *they* who exploited *you*, that it was *you*
who behaved outrageously, not they, that it was *you* who
defamed *them*, not they who defamed you, that *you* were
the traitor, and so on. I took into account all the reasons
for not visiting them; I could find none in favor of doing
so after being out of contact for twenty years, yet finally,
despite my repugnance, despite the immense hatred I bore
them, I made up my mind that I would visit them, and so
I slipped on my coat and set out for the Gentzgasse. I've
come to the Gentzgasse, I told myself, sitting in the wing
chair, even though it's the last thing I wanted to do.
Everything was against my coming to the Gentzgasse,
everything was against such a ludicrous *artistic dinner*, yet
now I'm here. *On the way to the Gentzgasse I kept saying to
myself, I'm against this visit, I'm against the Auersbergers, I'm
against all the people who are going to be there, I hate them, I
hate all of them. And yet I kept on walking and finally rang
the bell of their apartment.* Everything was against my
making an appearance in the Gentzgasse and yet I've
made it, I said to myself as I sat in the wing chair. And

again it occurred to me that I would have done better to
read my Gogol and my Pascal and my Montaigne, or to
play Schönberg or Satie, or just to take a walk through the
streets of Vienna. And in fact the Auersbergers were even
more surprised at my appearing in the Gentzgasse than I
was myself, I thought. I could tell this from the way
Auersberger's wife received me, and even more clearly
from the way Auersberger himself received me. You
shouldn't have come to the Gentzgasse, I told myself the
moment I found myself facing her. It's an act of insanity,
I told myself as I held out my hand to him. He didn't
shake it—whether this was because he was drunk or
because he was being abominably rude I can't say, I
thought, sitting in the wing chair. They issued their invitation in the Graben in the belief that I wouldn't come
under any circumstances, I thought, sitting in the wing
chair; perhaps they themselves didn't really know why
they invited me to their dinner, immediately referring to
it as an *artistic dinner*—which was a fatal mistake, I
thought, as it made them seem ridiculous. But the Auersbergers could have refrained from speaking to me in the
Graben, I thought; they could have ignored me, as they
had done for decades, just as I had ignored them for
decades, I thought, sitting in the wing chair. Joana's to
blame for this invitation, I thought, she's the cause of my
irrational behavior, the dead woman has this distasteful
contretemps on her conscience. Yet at the same time I
thought how nonsensical such an idea was, but it kept
coming back—again and again I had this nonsensical
notion that the dead Joana was to blame for that *irrational
reaction in the Graben*, which finally led to my coming to

the Gentzgasse, against my natural inclinations, to take part in this *artistic dinner*. It was because of Joana's death that as soon as the Auersbergers saw me in the Graben they canceled the past twenty years, during which we had had absolutely no contact with one another, and issued their invitation, and for the selfsame reason I accepted it. And then of course they added that they had *invited the Burgtheater actor*, who was *enjoying such a triumph in The Wild Duck*, as Auersberger's wife put it, and I said I would come. Never in the last ten or fifteen years have I accepted an invitation to a dinner at which an actor was to be one of the guests, I thought as I sat in the wing chair, never have I gone anywhere where an actor was going to be present, and then suddenly I'm told that an actor is coming to dinner—an actor from the Burgtheater at that, and what's more to a dinner party at the Auersbergers' apartment in the Gentzgasse—and I go along. There was no point now in clapping my hand to my forehead. Actually I'm doing nothing to hide the revulsion I feel for all these people, and for the Auersbergers themselves, I told myself as I sat in the wing chair; on the contrary they can all sense that I loathe and detest them. They can't just see that I hate them—they can hear it too. Conversely I had the impression that all these people were hostile to me; from what I saw of them and in everything I heard them say, I sensed their aversion, even their hatred. The Auersbergers hated me; they realized that I was the blemish they had wished on their dinner party by being so thoughtless as to invite me; they were dreading the moment when the actor would enter the apartment and they would ask us all to take our places at table and begin the meal. They

saw that I was the observer, the repulsive person who had
made himself comfortable in the wing chair and was playing his disgusting observation game in the semidarkness
of the anteroom, more or less *taking the guests apart*, as
they say. They had always found it offensive that I should
seize every opportunity of quite unscrupulously taking
them apart, but in mitigation, I told myself as I sat in the
wing chair, I could always plead that I took myself apart
much more often than anybody else, never sparing myself,
always dissecting myself *into all my component parts*, as
they would say, with equal nonchalance, equal vicious-
ness, and equal ruthlessness. In the end there was always
much less left of me than there was of them, I told myself.
I had one consolation: I was not the only one to curse the
fact that I had come to the Gentzgasse, that I had been
guilty of such imbecility and weakness of character—the
Auersbergers too were cursing themselves for inviting me.
But I was there, and nothing could be done about it.
Thirty years ago I used to share their apartment with
them, going in and out of it as though it were my own
home, I thought as I sat in the wing chair observing what
was happening in the music room, which was so brightly
lit that nothing could escape me, while I remained in the
dark all the time, occupying what was without doubt the
most favorable position I could possibly occupy in this
disagreeable situation. I had known all the guests at this
artistic dinner, as I had known the Auersbergers themselves, virtually for decades, except for the young people;
among these were two young writers, but they did not
interest me: I did not know them and so had no reason
whatever to concern myself with them, except to observe

them. I did not feel the slightest urge to go over and talk to them, to challenge them to a conversation or an argument. I was probably too tired, for I had been completely exhausted by the strain of the funeral, by what I had gone through in Kilb for Joana's sake, I thought, above all the dreadful scenes *after* the funeral, which were so incredible that I shall only gradually be able to take them in; I still did not have the necessary mental clarity to comprehend them, and I thought I would need a thorough sleep before I could even begin. Sitting in the wing chair I was already starting to think that when I got home I would go straight to bed and not get up for the whole of the following day and the following night, perhaps even the next day and the next night too—so exhausted, so *worn out* did I feel as I sat in the wing chair. We imagine we are twenty and act accordingly, yet in fact we are over fifty and completely exhausted, I thought; we treat ourselves like twenty-year-olds and ruin ourselves, and we treat everybody else as though we were all still twenty, even though we're fifty and can't stand the pace any longer; we forget that we have a medical condition, more than one in fact, a number of medical conditions, a number of so-called *fatal diseases*, but we ignore them for as long as we can and don't take them seriously, though they're there all the time and ultimately kill us. We treat ourselves as though we still had the strength we had thirty years ago, whereas in fact we don't have a fraction of our former strength, not even a fraction, I thought, sitting in the wing chair. Thirty years ago I would think nothing of staying up for two or three nights on end, drinking virtually non-stop, not caring what I drank, and performing like an *entertainment machine*, playing the fool for several nights—round the clock, as they say—for all sorts of people, all of them friends, without doing myself the slightest harm. For years, as it now seems, I never got home before three or four in the morning; I would go to bed with the dawn chorus, yet it didn't do me the slightest harm. For years I would turn up at the *Apostelkeller* or some other dive in the city around eleven in the evening and not leave before three or four in the morning, having used up every possible drop of energy, I may say, with the utmost ruthlessness, though it was a ruthlessness which at that time was second nature to me and, as it now seems, did me no harm at all. And I spent countless nights talking and drinking with Joana, I thought as I sat in the wing chair. I had no money or possessions of any kind, yet the truth is that for years I whiled away the nights talking, drinking and dancing with Joana and her husband, with Jeannie Billroth, and above all with the Auersbergers. In those days I had all the energy a young man could possibly have, and I had no scruples about letting myself be supported by anyone better off than myself, I recalled in the wing chair. I never had a penny in my pocket, yet I could afford whatever I wanted, I thought, sitting in the wing chair and observing the guests in the music room. And for years I would go out every day to the Simmeringer Hauptstrasse in the late afternoon to spend the night with Joana, calling at Dittrich's on the way to pick up the wine, and then return in the early morning, either catching the No. 71 or walking back to Währing along the Simmeringer Hauptstrasse, down the Rennweg, and across the Schwarzenbergerplatz. In those days, I recalled, horse-drawn carts could still be seen parked at night in front of the dairies, and it was still possible to walk down the middle of the Rennweg, cut across the Schwarzenbergplatz, and walk along the deserted Ring without being afraid of being run over. I seldom met another soul, and if I did it was sure to be one of my own kind—another late-night reveler—and it was a rarity to see a car cruising through the streets at that hour. Never in my life have I sung so many Italian arias as I did in those days as I walked from the Simmeringer Hauptstrasse to the Rennweg, then across the Schwarzenbergerplatz and back to Währing, I thought as I sat in the wing chair. At that time I had the strength to walk *and* sing; now I'm not even strong enough to *walk and talk*—that's the difference. Thirty years ago I thought nothing of a ten-mile walk home at night, I recalled in the wing chair, *singing all the way in my youthful enthusiasm for Mozart and Verdi and giving vent to my intoxication.* It's thirty years, I thought, since I made operatic history in this way—thirty years. The truth is, I thought, sitting in the wing chair, that my life would have taken a different course had it not been for Joana; perhaps I'd have pursued a diametrically opposed course had I not met Auersberger. For my encounter with Auersberger meant essentially a return to things artistic, on which I had turned my back completely—and definitively, as I then believed—after leaving the Mozarteum. At that time, after passing out of the Mozarteum, I suddenly wanted nothing more to do with the supposedly artistic, having opted firmly for the opposite of what I would call *the artistic,* but then my meeting with Auersberger, I recalled in the wing chair, caused me once more to do a complete about-turn. And

then I met Joana, I recalled, who was the quintessence of
everything artistic. It was for the artistic, not for art, that
I opted thirty-five years ago—only *the artistic,* I thought
as I sat in the wing chair, *though I had no idea what that
was.* I opted for *the artistic,* though I didn't know what
form it would take. I quite simply opted for Auersberger,
for Auersberger as he was then, thirty-five or thirty-four
years ago, and as he still was thirty-three years ago—for
the artistic Auersberger. And for Joana, the quintessentially
artistic Joana. And for Vienna. And for the artistic world,
I thought, sitting in the wing chair. I owe it to Auersberger that I executed an about-turn and returned to the
artistic world, I thought, sitting in the wing chair, and
above all I owe it to Joana—to everything that was connected with Auersberger and Joana thirty-five years ago,
and was still connected with them thirty-two years ago—
that's the truth, I thought, sitting in the wing chair. Several times I repeated to myself the words *the artistic world*
and *the artistic life.* I actually spoke them out loud, in such
a way that people in the music room were bound to hear
them—as indeed they did, for all their heads suddenly
turned in my direction, from the music room to the anteroom—though they could not actually see me—on hearing me repeating the words *the artistic life* and *the artistic
world.* I recalled what the notions *artistic world* and *artistic
life* had meant to me then, and still meant to me today—
more or less *everything,* I now thought, sitting in the wing
chair, and I thought how tasteless it was for the Auersbergers to call this dinner of theirs—or rather this supper—an *artistic dinner.* How low they've sunk, I thought
as I sat in the wing chair—these people who as far as I can

see have been artistically, intellectually and spiritually bankrupt for decades. But to all these people in the music room, hearing me utter the words *artistic world* and *artistic life*, it was of course as though I had said *artistic dinner* just as the Auersbergers might have done, and apart from being so audible they struck nobody as in any way unusual—nobody realized what they meant to me. At one time, of course, all these people had actually been artists, or at least possessed *artistic talents*, I thought, sitting in the wing chair, but now they were just so much *artistic riffraff*, having about as much to do with art and the artistic as this dinner party of the Auersbergers'. All these people, who were once real artists, or at least in some way artistic, I thought as I sat in the wing chair, are now nothing but shams, husks of their former selves: I have only to listen to what they say, I have only to look at them, I have only to come into contact with their products, to feel exactly the same way about them as I feel about this supper party, this tasteless *artistic dinner*. To think what has happened to all these people over the past thirty years, I thought, to think what they've made of themselves in these thirty years! And what I've made of myself in these thirty years! It's unrelievedly depressing to see what they've made of themselves, what I've made of myself. All these people have contrived to turn conditions and circumstances that were once happy into something utterly depressing, I thought, sitting in the wing chair; they've managed to make everything depressing, to transform all the happiness they once had into utter depression, just as I have. For there's no doubt that thirty or even twenty years ago all these people were happy, but now they're unutterably depressing, every bit as depressing and unhappy as I am myself, I thought as I sat in the wing chair. They've transformed sheer happiness into sheer misery, I thought, sitting in the wing chair, unalloyed hope into unrelieved hopelessness. For what I saw when I looked into the music room was a scene of unmitigated hopelessness, both human and artistic, I thought, sitting in the wing chair—that's the truth. All these people had come to Vienna in the fifties, thirty years earlier, some of them forty years earlier, hoping they would go far, as they say, but the farthest they *actually* went in Vienna was to become tolerably successful provincial artists, and the question is whether they would have gone any farther in any other so-called big city—*they* probably wouldn't have gone very far anywhere, I thought. But when I reflect that they've got nowhere in Vienna, nowhere at all, I thought, I also realize that they're unaware of this, for they don't act as though they were aware of having got nowhere: on the contrary they behave as though they'd gone far in Vienna, as though every one of them had become something worthwhile; they think that all the hopes they placed in Vienna have been fulfilled, I thought, or at least most of the time they believe they've gone far—most of the time they believe fervently that they've become something worthwhile, although from my point of view they haven't become anything. Because they've made *a name* for themselves, won *a lot of prizes*, published a lot of books, and sold their pictures to a lot of museums, because they've had their books issued by the best publishing houses and their pictures hung in the best museums, because they've been awarded every possible prize that this appalling state

has to offer and had every possible decoration pinned to
their breasts, they believe they've become something,
though in fact they've become nothing, I thought. They're
all what are termed *well-known artists, celebrated artists,*
who sit as senators in the so-called *Art Senate;* they call
themselves professors and have chairs at our academies;
they are invited by this or that college or university to
speak at this or that symposium; they travel to Brussels or
Paris or Rome, to the United States and Japan and the
Soviet Union and China, where sooner or later they're
invited to give lectures about themselves and open exhibi-
tions of their pictures, and yet as I see it they haven't
become anything. They've all quite simply failed to achieve
the highest, and as I see it *only the highest* can bring real
satisfaction, I thought. Auersberger's compositions don't
go unperformed, I thought, sitting in the wing chair;
*Auersberger, the successor of Webern, hasn't failed to gain rec-
ognition,* I thought. On the contrary, not a moment passes
without something of his being sung, without one of his
compositions being performed by brass, woodwind,
strings or percussion (he makes sure of that!)—now in
Basel, now in Zürich, now in London, now in Klagenfurt—here a duet, there a trio, here a four-minute chorus,
there a twelve-minute opera, here a three-minute cantata,
there a one-second opera, a one-minute song, a two-min-
ute or four-minute aria; sometimes he engages English
performers, sometimes French or Italian; sometimes his
work is performed by a Polish or Portuguese violinist,
sometimes by a Chilean or Italian lady on the clarinet.
Hardly has he arrived in one town than he's thinking
about the next, our restless successor of Webern, it seems,

our mincing, globe-trotting imitator of Webern and Grafen, our snobbish, musical dandy from the Styrian sticks. Just as Bruckner is unendurably monumental, so Webern is unendurably meager, yet the meagerness of Anton Webern is as nothing compared with the meagerness of Auersberger, whom I am bound to describe as the *almost noteless* composer, just as the mindless literary experts have dubbed Paul Celan the *almost wordless* poet. This Styrian imitator doesn't go unperformed, but thirty years ago, in the mid-fifties, he was already stuck in the Webern tradition; he's never written so much as three notes without making some composition or other out of them. What is missing in Auersberger's compositions, it seems to me, is Auersberger himself; his aphoristic music (which was how I described his derivative compositions in the fifties!) is nothing but an *unendurable copy* of Webern, who was himself, as I now realize, not the genius he was taken to be, but only a sudden—if brilliant—access of debility in the history of music. In fact I feel heartily ashamed of myself as I sit in the Auersbergers' wing chair and reflect that Auersberger was never a genius, even though back in the fifties I was utterly convinced that he was: he was simply a pathetic little bourgeois with a certain talent, who gambled away his talent in his first few weeks in Vienna. Vienna is a terrible machine for the destruction of genius, I thought, sitting in the wing chair, an appalling recycling plant for the demolition of talent. All these people whom I was now observing through their sickening cigarette smoke came to Vienna thirty or thirty-five years ago, hoping to go far, only to have whatever genius or talent they possessed annihilated and killed off by the city, which kills off all the hundreds and thousands of geniuses or talents that are born in Austria every year. They may think they've gone far, but in reality they haven't gone anywhere, I thought as I sat in the wing chair, and the reason is that they were content to stay in Vienna: they didn't leave at the decisive moment and go abroad, like all those who did achieve something; those who stayed behind in Vienna became nonentities, whereas I can say without hesitation that all those who went abroad made something of themselves. Because they were satisfied with Vienna, they ended up as nonentities, unlike those who left Vienna at the decisive moment and went abroad, I thought, sitting in the wing chair. I will not speculate about what might have become of all these people in the music room, all these people who were waiting around for the artist to make his entrance and for the *artistic dinner* to begin, if they had left Vienna at the crucial moment in their lives. It took no more than a minor success, a favorable press review of her first novel, to make Jeannie Billroth stay in Vienna, no more than the sale of a couple of pictures to national museums to make Rehmden the painter stay in Vienna, no more than a few fulsome notices in the *Kurier* or the *Presse* to persuade some promising actress to stay in Vienna. The music room is full of people who stayed on in Vienna, I thought as I sat in the wing chair. And at the cemetery in Kilb those who followed Joana's coffin were almost exclusively people who had stayed on in Vienna, almost suffocating in the comfort of their petit bourgeois world. What a depressing effect the funeral at Kilb had on me, for this reason more than any other! I thought, watching these people from the wing

chair. What depressed me was not so much the fact that
Joana was being buried as that the only people who followed her coffin were artistic corpses, failures, Viennese
failures, the living dead of the artistic world—writers,
painters, dancers and hangers-on, artistic cadavers not yet
quite dead, who looked utterly grotesque in the pelting
rain. The sight was not so much sad as unappetizing, I
thought. All through the ceremony I was obsessed by the
spectacle of these repellent artistic nonentities trudging
behind the coffin through the cemetery mud in their distasteful attitudes of mourning, I told myself as I sat in the
wing chair. It was not so much the funeral that aroused
my indignation as the demeanor of the mourners who had
turned up from Vienna in their flashy cars. I became so
agitated that I had to take several heart tablets, yet my
agitation was brought on not by the dead Joana, but by the
behavior of these arty people, these artistic shams, I
thought, and it occurred to me that my own behavior at
Kilb had probably been equally distasteful. The very fact
that I had put on a black suit was distasteful, I now told
myself; so was the way I had eaten my goulash in the *Iron
Hand* and the way I had talked to Joana's companion, as
though I were the only person who had really been close
to Joana, the only one who had any claim on her. The
more I thought about the funeral, the more I became
aware of the distasteful aspects of my own behavior: no
matter what circumstances came to mind, they were all
equally distasteful. Finding the others distasteful, I naturally could not help finding myself distasteful too, I
thought, and the more I thought about everything connected with the funeral, the more reprehensible my own

conduct seemed to me. It had been distasteful to go to
Kilb *alone*, despite the fact that several people had offered
to drive me there, I thought, and it had been distasteful to
talk to the woman from the general store, Joana's friend,
as though *I* had been closest to her; it had been inconsid-
erate to monopolize her company, leaving her no time to
attend to the other people who had come to the funeral, I
thought. *I* had made myself *the star of the funeral*, I thought,
and I now saw how monstrous this had been. I had down-
graded Joana's companion and all the others at the funeral
and at the same time upgraded myself—and that was
contemptible. On the other hand I had believed at the
time that I was behaving *properly*. During the funeral I
had been unaware of incurring any guilt: only now, sitting
in the wing chair, did I develop what might be called a
sense of guilt with regard to my conduct at Kilb. The fact
that Joana had killed herself did not make me feel any
sadder in Kilb, I thought, sitting in the wing chair: it simply aroused my indignation against her friends, though I
could not explain to myself why this should be. The truth
is that I was not in the least shocked to get the telephone
call from the owner of the general store, informing me
that Joana had committed suicide; I *pretended* to be
shocked, I now reflected, but in fact I wasn't—I was *curious, but not shocked*. I only *feigned* shock; I was merely curious and immediately wanted her to tell me everything
about Joana's suicide. I displayed the most outrageous
curiosity, and it was only now, sitting in the wing chair,
that I felt shocked by this—by the fact that I had not been
sad, but merely curious, and that I had forced more information out of the woman than she was willing to impart,

for during our telephone conversation she showed a decency that was entirely lacking in me. Naturally Joana had become such a stranger to me and we had been out of touch for so many years, that the call from the woman at the general store, as I have said, could not possibly have come as a shock, nor could it cause me any immediate sadness; it produced merely curiosity, and this curiosity forced her to tell me everything about Joana's suicide there and then. I was interested not in the fact of her suicide, but in the circumstances. I was *sad*. I was *really saddened*, and it was in this mood of sadness that I walked into town—to the Graben, the Kärntnerstrasse and the Kohlmarkt, then to the *Bräunerhof* in the Spiegelgasse, where I glanced through the *Corriere*, *Le Monde*, the *Zürcher Zeitung* and the *Frankfurter Allgemeine Zeitung*, as I had been in the habit of doing for years. Then, sickened by the newspapers, I went back to the Graben to buy myself a tie, but instead of buying a tie I ran into the Auersbergers, to be told once again about Joana's suicide. By now I knew much more about it than they did, yet I pretended to know nothing. I put on such an act of bewilderment that the couple must have felt I was shocked by Joana's suicide, whereas in fact I was only *feigning* shock. I had actually felt saddened by Joana's suicide as I walked back and forth in the city, and then, quite suddenly and quite shamelessly, I pretended to the Auersbergers that I was shocked by it. And just as my shock was feigned, so too was my acceptance of the invitation to their *artistic dinner*, because the whole of my conduct toward the Auersbergers during our meeting in the Graben was pure dissembling. Sitting in the wing chair, I reflected that I had *pretended* to be shocked by Joana's suicide and pretended to accept the Auersbergers' invitation to their *artistic dinner.* When I accepted it I was only pretending, I now thought, yet in spite of this I had acted upon it. The idea is nothing short of grotesque, I thought, yet at the same time it amused me. Actually I've always dissembled with the Auersbergers, I thought, sitting in the wing chair, and here I am again, sitting in their wing chair and dissembling once more: I'm not really here in their apartment in the Gentzgasse, I'm only pretending to be in the Gentzgasse, only pretending to be in their apartment, I said to myself. I've always pretended to them about everything—I've pretended to everybody about everything. My whole life has been a pretense, I told myself in the wing chair—the life I live isn't real, it's a simulated life, a simulated existence. My whole life, my whole existence has always been *simulated*—my life has *always been pretense*, never reality, I told myself. And I pursued this idea to the point at which I finally *believed* it. I drew a deep breath and said to myself, in such a way that the people in the music room were bound to hear it: *You've always lived a life of pretense, not a real life—a simulated existence, not a genuine existence. Everything about you, everything you are, has always been pretense, never genuine, never real.* But I must put an end to this fantasizing lest I go mad, I thought, sitting in the wing chair, and so I took a large gulp of champagne.

Translated by David McLintock

The Great Heat Wave

Jörg Mauthe

IT WASN'T LOVE that bound Dr. Tuzzi to Ulrike but sheer perversion, a quite innocent yet exquisite fetishism. Even though Ulrike was a beautiful and very elegant young lady, Tuzzi's desire had not at the time been aroused by the total woman. It was only the one quality or peculiarity out of the entire ensemble that still exerted a considerable stimulating effect on Tuzzi's libido. This peculiarity was of a linguistic nature. When she spoke

---

JÖRG MAUTHE (born in Vienna in 1924–died in Vienna in 1986) studied art history, German literature and archeology and received his doctorate in 1948. He began his career as a journalist and cultural critic and worked as cultural editor and program developer for the national radio and television station ORF until 1978 when he switched to a political career. In 1980 he founded the monthly magazine *Wiener Journal*, which still exists today. As a writer he followed the classical Austrian models Nestroy, Raimund, Musil, Joseph Roth, and Doderer. His eighteen books all deal humorously with aspects of life in Austria and especially in Vienna. Like his forebears, he attempted to capture the essence of the Austrian identity and way of life, once a major theme of Austrian writers that has lost its importance today as the country now increasingly thinks European in terms of the European Union.

---

or recounted a series of events, Ulrike made exclusive use of the imperfect, a tense tolerated only in written form in this country. She actually said "I said" or "didn't you say?" and "I slept" and "yes I walked there." And when she asked about her lover's disposition, she said: "How did things go today?"

In short, Ulrike was a German.

And in fact, the imperfect, which seems so unbearable to our ears when it issues like an order from the mouth of the German male, does not sound at all that bad in the speech of a pretty young German female. Quite the contrary, it endows her at times with something both decidedly Amazon-like and refreshing. The latter quality, however, has an artificial tinge like bath salts or room deodorants. For men who appreciate the deliberately artificial aspects about women, their lipsticks and eyeliners, perfume, coiffure, and high-heeled shoes, all of which shift the focal point to the sensual heights of luminous or silken synthetics, veiling and revealing—for men like Dr. Tuzzi who can appreciate the allure of the artwork a talented woman can become, this linguistic peculiarity that sounds so alien and artificial to the Austrian ear can mean a marked extension of pleasure. Vibrating in sympathy with the imperfect, the cortical organ becomes an erogenous zone conveying unknown delights.

Many of our compatriots will understand Dr. Tuzzi in this respect.

Tuzzi had met Ulrike at a so-called new wine party. This form of sociability, recently in fashion in Vienna, stems from the consideration that the drudgery of numerous single invitations can be rationally avoided by simultaneously inviting all of those friends and acquaintances at whose homes one has enjoyed a visit during the past year. At the same time it is an occasion to show to the whole world that one is on intimate terms with the whole world. Unfortunately, such parties tend by nature to bog down in complete boredom since one normally meets the same crowd of people there that one has seen under similar circumstances a few days before. One now finds one's self, come what may, forced into a conversation about how much or how little one enjoyed the previous party. . . .

The party in question, however, was from the beginning unexpectedly pleasant. The host had selected a charming tavern on the edge of Grinzing, a courtyard trimmed by walnut trees and oleander planters between the whitewashed walls of an old vintner's house. It was a mild evening. The relationship of atmospheric pressure, humidity, and temperature was in that ideal state of balance that is one of the most important requirements of happiness. This was the last time, however, since a warm and dry winter had followed that beautiful autumn, a winter that ushered in the great heat wave. In any case, a general gaiety prevailed, a playful good will on everyone's part even before the first drop of wine had been drunk. The guests wandered on their own initiative from table to table. Archenemies temporarily discovered sympathetic characteristics in each other and meeting old acquaintances on this evening was almost a pleasure. Tuzzi, too, moved about in good humor through the general merriment. After he had drunk the first quarter of a liter of wine, he sensed a lightness, a sheer agility of the soul and spirit otherwise alien to him, that for this very reason

now delighted him. He came upon Ulrike in this condition. She was sitting at her table alone and listening with
an obvious lack of comprehension to the lively chatter
around her. The conversation had already reached that
relaxed state in which insinuation replaces entire biog-
raphies and jokes are being told about other jokes. The
Viennese dialect, with the tiniest of vowel shadings, is
capable of coaxing a charming tribute or a highly malicious yet scarcely intelligible insult from one and the same
word. Sometimes they emerge simultaneously. Moreover,
when things are going really well with the right people
in the right mood, the conversation sometimes reaches
a plateau where language is useless and words begin to
play their own games. The relationship of the Austrian,
not only the Viennese, to language is thoroughly sensual,
sexual, even salacious. Infatuated by language, he caresses
or maltreats it, becomes aroused by it and savors the act of
exploiting it. He lets himself be carried away and, in his
turn, seduces it anew.

Perplexity, sometimes even vertigo, befalls the foreigner who stumbles into such an orgy of nuance. He
hears words and believes that he recognizes most of them
but at the same time senses his inability to comprehend
meanings that lie far behind, above and often enough,
below his linguistic horizon.

That's about the state in which Ulrike found herself on
that evening. Recognizing this and because he was bothered by such solitude in the midst of general merriment
as well as the fact of his natural attraction, Tuzzi took
his wine glass and sat down beside her. After they had

exchanged names he learned that she had just recently come to Vienna and had discovered this social set more or less by accident.

"A colleague told me I should come and I'd be sure to meet a lot of interesting people," she said.

The ossicles in Dr. Tuzzi's inner ear had already begun to vibrate pleasantly from the grammatically correct past tense and the High German subjunctive.

"But now I feel as if a group of the mentally deranged had been convened here," she continued candidly.

"You're quite right about that," the Councillor replied cheerfully. "There's no one here except the deranged. The little fat man over there, for example. . . ."

(A list of the guests at this point would run well beyond the limits of a chapter that is already in danger of falling apart. Since we would like to fabricate one anyway we will place it as a register at chapter's end. There it can either be read or skipped over.)

"I was right!" the girl exclaimed when Tuzzi had finished his malicious presentation and depiction of the other party guests. "They are deranged."

"Of course," Tuzzi said, "but, my dear, you should not draw any conclusions from it. There is something deranged about everything human. Just think about this, for example: man differs from all other beings, whether animal or angel, in that he always wants to be something other than he is."

"That's right," the girl said in the belief that she had finally understood at least something. "I, for example, would love to have become a grand courtesan."

"And if I might ask, why didn't you, my dear?"

"My goodness—I don't really know. Probably the wrong upbringing. But sometimes I dream. . . ."

"About what?"

"Well, simply that I were a courtesan."

The Councillor enjoyed her embarrassment at this confession although she seemed quite self-assured and, like magazine mannequins selling youthful exuberance, even a bit hardened. With a series of rapid but methodical side-glances he had in fact enjoyed everything that he had noted in the course of the last few minutes. She had long brown hair, very symmetrical facial features, adequately firm breasts, and hands which did not altogether fit her slightly masculine type but which looked surprisingly delicate and gentle. Tuzzi observed with regret that nothing could be ascertained about her legs because of the long, colorful garden dress.

"I appreciate your candidness," Tuzzi said craftily. "And I don't doubt for a minute that as a courtesan you would cast Pompadour, Merode, Cleopatra, and all of the real and fake countesses of Auersperg into the deepest shade if, let's say, circumstances had been different. But. . . ."

"Really now . . .," Ulrike interrupted him, "was that meant as a compliment?"

Oh my, Tuzzi thought, unfortunately she seems a little slow. But there's nothing wrong with that. After all, I don't want . . . —or do I? Well, I guess we'll just wait and see.

"A compliment? I'd be quite happy if you'd take it that way. But I really only said it because I'd assumed you had expected me to say it."

"But if I expected that . . . I'm completely mixed up again."

"Doesn't matter at all," Tuzzi added generously. "For the context it's only important that you too, a creature from a distant land . . ."

"From Düsseldorf."

" . . .from a very distant land, sometimes feel the urge to be something a little bit different than what you are. As someone once said, probably even Napoleon at times wished he were not Napoleon but a tall, blond, and slightly degenerate aristocrat instead. Henry Kissinger too must certainly at times dream of appearing as charming and highly aristocratic as Metternich in his day. I can also very easily imagine a captain of industry building in his fantasy life a tiny cabin on the forest's edge far away from the turmoil and ambitions of the world."

"Yes, that's right!" Ulrike exclaimed eagerly. "My father is just that kind."

"You see, you see! And wouldn't this kind of dream be enough in itself to give human existence a slightly deranged touch?" . . .

At this moment the Councillor was interrupted by a vigorous slap on the shoulder, a regrettable interruption since it would really have been very interesting to hear what an Embassy Councillor on assignment to the Interministerial Committee for Special Questions, especially under these stimulating conditions, would have added about the connection between history and mental derangement. The cause of the interruption was a fashionably tipsy, highly placed diplomat from the Foreign Ministry, Tuzzi's former boss. It was the man to whom

Tuzzi owed his committee assignment and who was once again intent upon renewing Tuzzi's obligations by simply pulling the Councillor away by the coattail in order to introduce him to the Chancellor. . . .

The consequences brought about by even the slightest contact with power are unpredictable and at times remarkable. One of the effects in Dr. Tuzzi's case was the sudden decision to intensify the relationship with Ulrike to adulterous dimensions. After all, Dr. Tuzzi reasoned, an evening so pleasantly begun needed a crowning culmination in order to reach true perfection.

He set out on his way back from the Chancellor in a state of excited expectation. In passing he stumbled into a conversational collision with a man whose most ardent wish for the past fifteen years had been to become a television director, a goal he would certainly not attain even in the next fifteen years. In Vienna success is attainable in any career except in the one most eagerly desired. And who should he bump into next?

"Hello Tuzzi!"

"Hello Trotta! I should have known that you would be here too!"

"Only by accident, purely by accident. Don't you want to introduce me to that charmer you . . ."

"Out of the question. Bye-bye Trotta!"

Cleverly using the trunk of a chestnut tree as cover and bypassing a group of acquaintances Tuzzi slipped the three musicians a large tip with instructions to come straightaway to his table. When he finally reached Ulrike again he found that an interloper from an old aristocratic family (employed in advertising) had taken

the seat next to her, obviously intent on crowning his
own evening. Tuzzi drove him away with the message
that his wife (a yoga teacher) was looking for him. This
was a particularly mean trick since Tuzzi had noticed
in one of the darker corners of the courtyard that the
lady in question was just about to engage in exercises
with a virile Styrian playwright, exercises that looked
more like some robust Alpine custom than an Indian
discipline.

"I didn't think you were coming back!" Ulrike said with
a reproach in her voice. She immediately added: "Were
you really serious about what you said earlier?"

"Probably not," Tuzzi replied. He no longer had any
idea what he might have said earlier and he had no desire
to talk about anything that didn't directly move the events
of the evening along toward its intended high point and
conclusion.

"But it sounded so serious," Ulrike said in a disappointed
and confused tone. "And just as if you had thought about
it a thousand times already and as if I were the first person
to hear about it from you."

"That's quite possible," Tuzzi said and was on the look-
out for an entry or an opening in her puzzlement that
he could pursue directly to the culminating ceremony.
"When a woman has such intelligent eyes and can listen
as well as you can, a man says things that he would otherwise only think . . ."

Tuzzi knew that was crude, even primitive and he
was a bit ashamed. An intelligent woman of these parts
would, if I were lucky, make fun of me and despise me if
my luck didn't hold. But Ulrike, who came from an area

where the spoken word was taken much more seriously, was promptly taken in by Tuzzi.

"That was nice," she said.

"What's that?"

"Well, what you just said—and it was quite charming too."

There it was—the opening. And there was the verbal pistol shot that signaled the Councillor—to express it in a fashionable image—to spring out of his starting block and make the mad dash toward his goal. Attesting to an Austrian's charm doesn't simply mean baring one's breast to an open sword but rushing posthaste into the open blade. When it's a question of making use of this characteristic the Austrian knows no mercy! What a pity, for example, when a meeting of German-Austrian dignitaries is opened by a reception "with the ladies." The spectacle of the Austrian contingent kissing the hands of the German ladies with an air of icy brutality simply must be seen firsthand to be believed! The mixture of envy and contempt in the looks of the German men must be observed as well as the enchanted reactions of the ladies who are both enthralled and humiliated. Humiliated because in their near total ignorance about having their hand kissed, they have not relaxed their wrists and fingers quickly enough between the accustomed handshake and the unexpected hand kiss. They now imagine themselves to be clumsy and dull, completely helpless and at the mercy of the savoir-vivre of ancient tradition. Many a round of negotiation embarked on in this way has taken an incongruously favorable course for Tuzzi's countrymen right from the beginning.

"Charming?" the Councillor said. "Not at all, not at all. It wasn't charm that you heard but on the contrary—please excuse the word—it was pure, unadulterated blather to which I gave free reign."

"Excuse me?"

"You don't understand the word and actually I shouldn't even use it since it belongs to a dialect level to which federal civil servants from the rank of chief executive officer upward need not descend. For them it is in fact called charm. From the rank of section chief on it's even called diplomacy. I see the question reflected in those intelligent eyes gazing sweetly but confused into mine—let me explain to you what this hideous sounding word means. It's a method for inducing one party in a dialogue to some change, whether it involves an action, a conviction or even a mood. It does not function by rational argumentation, but rather by the pretense of arguments that may or may not be substantial. I'm not saying that blather—I regret having to utter this repugnant word yet one more time—is the same as lying although they have a lot in common. One of its devices, for example, is endowing the truth with the appearance of falsehood while, on the other hand, it readily uses a manifest lie as a reflection of an apparent truth. This linguistic folk art dances merrily along on the razor's edge between truth and untruth, holding mirror up to mirror, seldom heading for a definite goal and often merely reflecting its own narcissistic image in all the mirror surfaces. Evading every attempt to pin it down, it depicts possibility as reality, reality as the shadow of unreality . . . I see that you don't understand me, but I don't know how I can make all of this clear to a beautiful alien from an area where one doesn't say in German 'have said' but rather 'said,' where one doesn't say 'have slept,' but where one says 'slept'—or better yet 'slept together.' It's as if one would clearly and beyond all doubt like to assert and testify to things when they are already forgotten, passé, and removed to the past. But I digress and you probably don't even understand that for some time I've been declaring my love for you as well as making an immoral suggestion. Moreover, at this point I honestly don't know if language itself has led me into this situation—careful with the word 'honestly'!—or whether, as I hope, it's not been language but reality. No, I see that you don't understand, but it is lovely how you've allowed me to hold your hand, a hand that has something surprisingly girlish about it, a hint of innocence in striking contrast to the 'imperfect' chic and clarity of your beautiful appearance. Perhaps you shouldn't drink any more, my dear, bewildered alien. This wine is light only for those unfamiliar with it. Listen instead to the musicians who are playing a so-called old dance. Listen, if you will, to these experts of musical blather playing a basically straightforward melody in such a wistful and perplexing way, playing it so that it evokes for me, and perhaps as I say it, for you, the image of an inebriated figure staggering blissfully and mute across a sunny forest clearing . . . Precisely as I had hoped, lovely victim of my amorality, I note that this melody affects your ear more favorably than my words or is it perhaps the way the notes are alternately held and cut short? Shall we go?"

And thus Dr. Tuzzi crowned his evening in the way he had intended and hoped. In judicious restriction of our means, means that will have to be strained toward the end of the story, we wish to eliminate the details of this culminating experience. And there is nothing much to be reported about them. Ulrike was certainly a grand courtesan only in her dreams yet gave the Councillor no reason to regret his decision. Guided by the firm resolve to perform conscientiously and to complete everything undertaken in the most thorough and consummate manner possible, she proved herself worthy of her origins. In the end she not only set off vibations in the ossicles of Dr. Tuzzi's inner ear but in his heart as well.

And if there was something that bothered him a little about the whole affair it was Ulrike's final comment, a comment intended as a sign of affection:

"You know, it was really sweet how you exerted yourself, but things would have been the same without all of your talking. I wanted to sleep with you anyway from the moment I saw you."

—Translated by Francis Michael Sharp

The Curse II
Rose Ausländer

A SUNDAY IN JULY. The sky was uniformly gray-blue. A haze, not clouds. At 8:00 the sun was already beating down. My prognosis was that it would be hot and humid, but up on the Kahlenberg and the Leopoldsberg, more than 1,500 feet above Vienna, it will be as cool as in the woods. I wanted to be alone, to have uninterrupted time

ROSE AUSLÄNDER (born in Czernowitz, Bukowina, in 1907–died in Düsseldorf, Germany in 1988) studied philosophy and literature. She remained steadfast in her attachment to Austria, and no matter where she lived, she always regarded Vienna as her home. She emigrated to America in 1921, became a citizen in 1926, and returned to Czernowitz in 1931. Highly gifted and versatile as a writer, she became a prominent member of the literary circle in Czernowitz and Bukarest and published her first book *Der Regenbogen* (*The Rainbow*) in 1939. When the Soviets retreated before the advancing German troops in 1941, they invited all Jewish citizens to leave with them. She decided to remain and suffered a harsh life of persecution in prison camps under the Nazis during World War II. In 1946 she moved to New York, where she supported herself with difficulty as a translator and foreign correspondent, and then moved to Düsseldorf in 1966. Her *Collected Works*, consisting of novels, short prose narratives, and poetry, were published in 7 volumes in 1984–1988.

for the problem that had been troubling me for a long time. And to write. I took my notebook with me.

At 10:30 I was in Grinzing, at the foot of the Kahlenberg. The charm of this area, with its ornate fountains, steep, narrow streets, and precious little Austrian-yellow houses is as strong as ever. In summer Grinzing is the hub of the city's night life, the most popular evening attraction. "Genuine Viennese atmosphere" is presented here. A casual evening in an outdoor "Heurigen," with local wine accompanied by the strings of a zither and folk songs in Viennese dialect, is a ritual to which just about every tourist subjects himself.

It took the packed bus about twenty minutes to wind its way up to the top of the Kahlenberg. Soon I was standing on the observation terrace. The two comfortable benches weren't there. Why? Why is Vienna, famous for its gemütlichkeit, getting less and less gemütlich? The city below seemed to be sleeping under a milk-white veil—a hazy pattern, marked by glittering golden towers. Dissolved in pastel reflections, it glistened like a painting from Monet's last period. Not a line that marked a distinct boundary was clearly visible, not even the towers of St. Stephen's Cathedral and the Votive Church. To the left, winding, threadlike flashes of light suggested the course of the Danube. Frothy green waves framed the picture.

This city that moves in circles—the streets around the center, the "ring" and the long "belt," and the circle of woods—wasn't this roundish Vienna a waltz motif? Even the plump people, the soft accent, the melodic voices. Was it an accident that the waltz made its home here, that Johann Strauss created his melodies in three-quarter time in this city? Vienna's façade is a waltz, I thought, but is that the whole story? Isn't there also a more sharply defined profile of Vienna, an independently minded center of the city with stronger lines? It was asleep for a long time. It is beginning to awaken. Fresh breezes are blowing across the literary landscape. The other arts, too, are on the upswing, with expanded horizons.

Noisy, colorful signs of life flooded the terrace. Several languages flitted through the air. Some I understood, others were at least identifiable. Two Japanese women, no less charming than their fascinating language, were speaking softly. I caught snippets of English, French, Hungarian, Romanian, North German, Swiss German, Slavic, and Scandinavian languages. Vienna has become a city of tourists. But a city of importance? No, a large provincial city: it shuts down at 9:00 P.M.—at night the streets are virtually deserted. This richly ornate, rose-scented capital city of Austria still manifests its baroque character in the downtown area—in spite of a number of modern buildings that disturb the mood—and some of the outlying areas retain their idyllic charm. The typical Viennese is a provincially minded chauvinist. He is thoroughly lovable, almost painfully polite, as long as he is met with an equally courtly gallantry, and his chauvinistic feelings are not hurt. If the customary ceremoniousness is not properly respected he raises his quills—a disguised porcupine—attacks, becomes nasty and vicious. The typical Viennese is Janus-faced: courtly and malicious, submissive and arrogant, sanguine and hysterical. The typical Viennese does not let someone who is not from his city, from his country, get close to him; he hermetically seals himself off from outsiders. No, the "typical" Viennese is an abstraction—he is as I have described, but he is also different.

With thoughts like these running through my mind I set off for the Leopoldsberg. There, in the restaurant garden with the enchanting panoramic view, I hoped to spend several quiet hours.

A broad path leads through the woods from the Kahlenberg to the Leopoldsberg. The tall trees, in full foliage, provide ample shade. Even familiar things can catch your eye. As usual the forested landscape made its fascination felt. The acoustical and visual effect of the movement of the leaves took hold of me. Innumerable blackbirds, thrushes, and other birds that never grow tired of singing make their home here in the loosely woven ceiling of this gigantic room. At first I concentrated on individual trees, but as the different shades of green passed by, the trees faded together, producing a unity and a union, a single form: the forest.

Then a striking rhythm took hold of me. It was the melody of the Yiddish singer Hertz Grossbart to the lyrics of "Waltz" by Lutzky. An anti-waltz emerges from the harsh quality of the melody. The song begins with the words "One two three." I enjoyed half-marching to this rhythm, rigid and yet strangely airy, the melody relieved my body of some of its weight. Countless voices accompanied me with repeated 1-2-3 variations. The melodic figures came together, floated apart, flew together again, and became entangled in an improvised atonal score.

Suddenly I had to stop. Something touched my back. It wasn't anything concrete. Two waves, a few inches apart, touched my back and made a circle on it. I did not want to turn around. No distractions today, I commanded myself, and resumed my 1-2-3 tempo. Then I heard steps next to me and felt the same two ghostly sensations on my left cheek. I turned my head to the right, quickened my pace, and reached level ground in a few minutes. I walked through the large gate, angled to the left, and entered the long, narrow terrace on the Leopoldsberg.

Here, too, the shock of the familiar: the spectacular panorama to the south and to the east. As before, the nebulous outlines of Vienna lay motionless in the whitish haze under the numbing heat, raised patches of green scattered on the silvery glistening plain. The Danube, a winding silvery line, shone dimly. To the left: the solid Bisamberg, the wooded hills descending to Klosterneuburg. Above and to the right the Kahlenberg assumed a defiantly angular pose, a colossus in green plumage. And up above hung the bell, cornflower-blue, whose golden clapper dreamily radiated downward.

I breathed a sigh of relief. The pressure on my back and cheek was no longer there. Maybe it had only been a figment of my imagination or a product of the enchanting melody. I was alone with the landscape, with the blackbird Sunday, with my thoughts.

There were the two waves again, boring into my cheek like screws. In consternation I ran back to the end of the terrace, through the court into the restaurant, without breaking stride looked for a shady table with a view, and when I saw that the corner table at the left of the first row was being vacated, I ran to it and grabbed the back of the right-hand chair. Simultaneously a woman plopped down in the chair facing me, chuckled with pleasure, and cried: "Well, it looks like we've got the best table in the house!" I stood there and stared at her. What does she mean, WE! I didn't invite her. I want my privacy.

She was an older woman wearing old-fashioned clothes. Her dark hair had almost completely turned gray, most of her front teeth were missing, her cheeks were sunken. She rolled her dark eyes down toward the city, and then back up to me. "Why don't you take a seat?" she gushed, "don't you like it here? It really couldn't be prettier. Or should we find another table?" That WE again! I was confused, angry. My knees were shaking, I had to sit down. This obnoxious individual! Like a pair of shears her eyes were shredding my precious privacy. I'll stay here five minutes and then move to another table, I decided—but, I immediately thought, that would be impolite. All right, half an hour, not a minute longer, I'm hungry, I'll have a bite while I'm here.

"Unfortunately I can only chat with you for a short time," I said, "I've got some work to do, some writing, it's pressing, I have to be alone." She laughed. "You can't be serious, who on earth comes *here* to work, especially on a Sunday like this? You can do that in the evening at home. Writing may be important, but a person is more important—and I am a person, right? I am Marie Krumholz. Today is my sixtieth birthday." I admitted defeat. A person is more important. The sixtieth birthday of a lonely person is more important. I offered my congratulations.

The waiter came, I ordered two soft-boiled eggs and a yogurt. Mrs. Krumholz asked for a small glass of beer and pulled a ham sandwich out of her purse. "I am so happy to be here today, I haven't been in the Vienna Woods for years—no time, work hard all week and then I've got to do everything myself at home—Sundays I just collapse. It's wonderful here, with you. We won't be bored." She pulled me deeper into that WE, I felt the magnetic power of her will.

"Are you a lawyer?" she asked and looked beseechingly at me. I shook my head. "Too bad!"—she sighed deeply— "I need an honest lawyer. Those scoundrels—lawyers— have robbed me of two inheritances. The second one could still be salvaged, but where can I find a decent lawyer? They just don't exist anymore. You have an honest face, I think I could trust you. When I caught sight of you on the Kahlenberg I thought to myself: this woman could help me obtain justice, maybe she is a lawyer, and so I followed you here. But I was wrong. You are Jewish, aren't you?" "Yes," I responded curtly. She said, "I am too—that is, actually I am Catholic, my father was Catholic and so was his wife, but my mother was Jewish. It was like this: my father's wife and a Jewess gave birth to baby girls on the same day and in the same hospital. Both mothers died the next day. The babies were inadvertently exchanged, as my father learned years later from a nun who was a nurse at the hospital. And so I am the child of a Jewish mother. Naturally my father brought me up as a Catholic, but I also received instruction in the Jewish religion, secretly. My father even took me to the synagogue, and he gave me a Jewish name, too: Miriam. I am a religious person. On Sunday I go to church and on the sabbath I often go to the synagogue. I fast on Yom Kippur. I love my people, Israel." And she pulled out a thin gold chain from under her blouse: a small gold cross and a Star of David hung from it. When I looked at her with astonishment she added: "It's the same God, isn't it?"

My curiosity had been aroused. "How did you live during the Hitler years? Did you wear the Star of David?" I asked, looking into her black, rolling eyes. They returned my gaze. "I was not persecuted, remember I am officially Catholic and was able to provide documentation of that fact. I sewed the Star of David into my purse, it was my talisman." "And the inheritances?" I inquired. "That happened later—complicated affairs, I lost the first case in 1955 and the second a short time ago. The lawyers conspired against me. But I got my revenge, I have already killed two of them."

I had difficulty catching my breath. A murderess? No, she didn't look like one. This wandering gaze, which suddenly and hypnotically turned to stone, her sudden movements, the mysterious litigation about the inheritances, and the two alleged murders: everything pointed to some kind of mental illness. She guessed my thoughts: "No, I am not crazy, it's a fact: I am responsible for the deaths of the two treacherous villains."

"What do you mean you are responsible?"

"I put a *curse* on them. People I put curses on are goners. My neighbor can vouch for it. When we were coming out of church together I said to her: all right, now I've put a *curse* on lawyer H., he won't live long. Three days later she comes running up to me and shows me an obituary in the newspaper: lawyer H. lost his life in an automobile accident. The other lawyer also died on the third day after I put my *curse* on him."

This woman clearly suffered from delusions. Her eyes bored into mine. "You don't believe me, you think I'm crazy, don't you?" I was glad that the waiter brought the food and interrupted the conversation. I wanted to avoid answering her questions so I asked: "You put a curse on your enemies in *church* and God heard you—how do you explain that?" "Very simple," she said, "after all, God is my father and I am his child. I didn't sin, steal, lie, commit adultery—I am pure. Now if I, his sinless child, put a curse on a villain, my father recognizes that I am in the right and complies with my request."

How can I get rid of her, I asked myself, and she responded, as though I had said it out loud: "Please don't go yet, I would like to share a secret with you: *I* destroyed HIM!"

"Whom, God?" I cried.

"No, how can you say such a thing—HITLER, of course," she answered and looked at me reproachfully. I cast a quick glance at her purse, she caught it and laughed in merriment. "Don't be concerned—here," and she opened her purse and showed it to me. "No, I don't carry my weapon in my purse. My weapon is the *curse*. God gave it to me on *that* day. My weapon is in there," and she pointed to her heart with her right hand.

Her eyes sparkled, she looked younger, her cheeks were red and full. She gave forth a magnetic impulse that arched over to me. "On what day did God give you the power of the curse?" I asked in a subdued tone. She closed her eyes and said: "It was like this: during those years I naturally had to conceal my Jewish birth, but I suffered along with my brothers and sisters. I learned about what was happening in the death camps from a woman who had worked in Auschwitz. Year by year I suffered with my tortured people until I couldn't stand it any longer. Then I began a hunger strike."

"Where, in prison?"

"No, at home—a hunger strike against God. I prayed, cried, and threatened him: 'I won't eat anything until you give me the gift of the CURSE. Lord, give me the power to destroy HIM with a CURSE, the power to save my people.' I fasted for seven days, drank only a couple swallows of water. On the seventh day I was no longer able to get out of bed. Then it happened. Very clearly a voice spoke in my ear: 'CHOOSE—CURSE or BLESSING!' Three times the voice repeated it, then silence. I chose the CURSE. It entered me immediately, a tremendous force. I felt stronger, I threw my clothes on and ran to church. On my knees I uttered the *curse*, three times, with all my power. Then I fell unconscious. I woke up in the hospital, I had good treatment, two days later I was able to go home. On the following day, that is, three days after the *curse*, my people were saved from Satan."

As in a dream I listened to her. Her fanatical faith in her miraculous curse—faith that moves mountains— infected me as well. "So we owe our lives to you," I said in all seriousness. At that point her intuition failed her. "You are mocking me," she cried bitterly, "I thought you were different from these straw men with no hearts, I thought you would see that I am another human being. Yes, God in his grace bestowed the *curse* upon me—yes, the surviving Jews owe their lives to me, and that includes you. It was through me that God destroyed the Hitler-Satan, and with God's help I got rid of those two rascals." I did not respond. After a while she said very softly, with her face turned away: "I know I sinned when I cursed the lawyers, but I couldn't help it."

Hesitantly I asked her: "Tell me, Mrs. Krumholz, why didn't you ask for the *blessing* when you had the choice?"

"But first my people had to be saved from their arch-enemy, don't you understand?" she screamed and banged her fist on the table. Totally mesmerized by her story, told with compelling conviction and accompanied by lively gestures, I fell into her mode of argumentation by accepting as incontrovertible fact the premise of the sacred origin of her curse. "Wouldn't Hitler have been powerless against God's blessing? Would he then still have been able to persecute our people?" was my question.

She grimaced. Wrathful bolts of lightning flashed from her eyes into mine. She hissed: "You have no right to reproach me for that! My blessing would not have had enough Power to save an entire people. But to destroy *one* person, just *one* mind you, my *curse* was adequate."

We both fell silent and turned to the landscape, I to the right and Marie-Miriam to the left. The layer of haze had disappeared. Gray blocks of apartment buildings with sharp contours had become visible, the Danube formed a dull, crooked line through the picture. The space between the sky and the valley below was also dull. Dark gray cloud clusters, like swollen stomachs, hung low in the sky. Thunderclaps rolled toward us from the distance. I called the waiter.

When we reached the path in the woods there was lightning above us. Sobered by her persistent silence, I mumbled that we would have to hurry if we wanted to reach the Kahlenberg before the rain started. Once again the 1-2-3 rhythm took control of me. Then something happened that took my breath away: very clearly it came from her lips: "la la la"—*my* melody. These three sounds from Marie-Miriam's mouth had a more profound effect on me than her story about the curse and the three murders. At first I had taken it for an obsession, a product of her imagination, then, in the dreamlike state that followed, as a gripping legend. But the la-la-la was reality, I heard it. Who was this little, old, ugly woman? A prophetess? "What was that you just sang?" I stammered. "Sang? Oh, I don't know, a melody just occurred to me." And she repeated unambiguously "la la la": *my* motif! Isn't that a miracle, like her curse, I asked myself.

It had gotten very dark, almost pitch-black. Suddenly Miriam-Marie slapped my face. "So I should have asked for the blessing? And not first saved my people from Satan?" And she ran a few steps ahead of me. Although she had not hit me hard, I stumbled. My cheek did not hurt, I only felt the outline of her hand on my face like electric impulses. Humiliated and totally disoriented I followed her.

In single file we quickly traversed the long dark path. The first drops fell just before we reached the hill. Then Miriam-Marie threw herself at me and embraced me. "Forgive me, forgive me, for God's sake! You are right. I've known it since that day, but I didn't want to admit it. It was very painful, hearing it from your lips—my damnation. You were the prosecutor, not my defense attorney—or are you perhaps representing God in this case?" The thunder storm descended on us in all its fury. Marie-Miriam did not loosen her grip on me. "I intended to go to the church on the Kahlenberg to curse you, but I cannot—cannot curse any more. The power of the curse has abandoned me, I am completely drained. The *blessing*! I will again fast for seven days. Farewell!" she mumbled, and as the rain beat down she ran up the last stairs and across the stretch of level ground, and entered the little church to the left, which was open.

Drenched to the skin I caught my bus.

—Translated by Jerry Glenn

A Hunger Artist

Franz Kafka

IN THE LAST DECADES interest in hunger artists has declined considerably. Whereas in earlier days there was good money to be earned putting on major productions of this sort under one's own management, nowadays that is totally impossible. Those were different times. Back then the hunger artist captured the attention of the entire city.

FRANZ KAFKA (born in 1883 in Prague–died in 1924 in outskirts of Vienna) is one of the best-known authors of Austrian and world literature. He took his law degree in 1906 to please his father, a successful businessman, who traumatized the boy, as Kafka described in 1919 in *Brief an den Vater* (*Letter to My Father*). His work in an accident insurance company also preyed on him, as he saw the pitiable people being shunted from office to office trying to find the person who might help them. These experiences form the basis of most of his short prose as well as his novels such as *Der Prozess* (*The Trial*) and *Das Schloss* (*The Castle*). Kafka describes peaceful individuals who live a contented, supposedly secure existence, only to be confronted suddenly by unfathomable and uncontrollable circumstances that pull them out of their secure world and permit no return. In the parable *The Hunger Artist* Kafka affirms life in the form of the healthy panther and a dying man's admission that he would have eaten, had he found the food he liked.

From day to day while the fasting lasted, participation increased. Everyone wanted to see the hunger artist at least daily. During the final days there were people with subscription tickets who sat all day in front of the small barred cage. And there were even viewing hours at night, their impact heightened by torchlight. On fine days the cage was dragged out into the open air, and then the hunger artist was put on display particularly for the children. While for grown-ups the hunger artist was often merely a joke, something they participated in because it was fashionable, the children looked on amazed, their mouths open, holding each other's hands for safety, as he sat there on scattered straw—spurning a chair—in a black tights, looking pale, with his ribs sticking out prominently, sometimes nodding politely, answering questions with a forced smile, even sticking his arm out through the bars to let people feel how emaciated he was, but then completely sinking back into himself, so that he paid no attention to anything, not even to what was so important to him, the striking of the clock, which was the single furnishing in the cage, merely looking out in front of him with his eyes almost shut and now and then sipping from a tiny glass of water to moisten his lips.

Apart from the changing groups of spectators there were also constant observers chosen by the public—strangely enough they were usually butchers—who, always three at a time, were given the task of observing the hunger artist day and night, so that he didn't get something to eat in some secret manner. It was, however, merely a formality, introduced to reassure the masses, for those who understood knew well enough that during the period of fasting the hunger artist would never, under any circumstances, have

eaten the slightest thing, not even if compelled by force.
The honour of his art forbade it. Naturally, none of the
watchers understood that. Sometimes there were nightly
groups of watchers who carried out their vigil very laxly,
deliberately sitting together in a distant corner and putting
all their attention into playing cards there, clearly intend-
ing to allow the hunger artist a small refreshment, which,
according to their way of thinking, he could get from some
secret supplies. Nothing was more excruciating to the hunger artist than such watchers. They depressed him. They
made his fasting terribly difficult. Sometimes he overcame
his weakness and sang during the time they were observing, for as long as he could keep it up, to show people how
unjust their suspicions about him were. But that was little
help. For then they just wondered among themselves about
his skill at being able to eat even while singing. He much
preferred the observers who sat down right against the bars
and, not satisfied with the dim backlighting of the room,
illuminated him with electric flashlights. The glaring light
didn't bother him in the slightest. Generally he couldn't
sleep at all, and he could always doze under any lighting
and at any hour, even in an overcrowded, noisy auditorium.
With such observers, he was very happily prepared to spend
the entire night without sleeping. He was very pleased to
joke with them, to recount stories from his nomadic life
and then, in turn, to listen their stories—doing everything
just to keep them awake, so that he could keep showing
them once again that he had nothing to eat in his cage and
that he was fasting as none of them could.

He was happiest, however, when morning came and a
lavish breakfast was brought for them at his own expense,
on which they hurled themselves with the appetite of

healthy men after a hard night's work without sleep. True, there were still people who wanted to see in this breakfast an unfair means of influencing the observers, but that was going too far, and if they were asked whether they wanted to undertake the observers' night shift for its own sake, without the breakfast, they excused themselves. But nonetheless they stood by their suspicions.

However, it was, in general, part of fasting that these doubts were inextricably associated with it. For, in fact, no one was in a position to spend time watching the hunger artist every day and night, so no one could know, on the basis of his own observation, whether this was a case of truly uninterrupted, flawless fasting. The hunger artist himself was the only one who could know that and, at the same time, the only spectator capable of being completely satisfied with his own fasting. But the reason he was never satisfied was something different. Perhaps it was not fasting at all which made him so very emaciated that many people, to their own regret, had to stay away from his performance, because they couldn't bear to look at him. For he was also so skeletal out of dissatisfaction with himself, because he alone knew something that even initiates didn't know—how easy it was to fast. It was the easiest thing in the world. About this he did not remain silent, but people did not believe him. At best they thought he was being modest. Most of them, however, believed he was a publicity seeker or a total swindler, for whom, at all events, fasting was easy, because he understood how to make it easy, and then had the nerve to half admit it. He had to accept all that. Over the years he had become accustomed to it. But this dissatisfaction kept gnawing at his insides all the time and never yet—and this one had to say to his credit—had he left the cage of his own free will after any period of fasting.

The impresario had set the maximum length of time for the fast at forty days—he would never allow the fasting go on beyond that point, not even in the cosmopolitan cities. And, in fact, he had a good reason. Experience had shown that for about forty days one could increasingly whip up a city's interest by gradually increasing advertising, but that then the people turned away—one could demonstrate a significant decline in popularity. In this respect, there were, of course, small differences among different towns and among different countries, but as a rule it was true that forty days was the maximum length of time.

So then on the fortieth day the door of the cage—which was covered with flowers—was opened, an enthusiastic audience filled the amphitheatre, a military band played, two doctors entered the cage, in order to take the necessary measurements of the hunger artist, the results were announced to the auditorium through a megaphone, and finally two young ladies arrived, happy about the fact that they were the ones who had just been selected by lot, seeking to lead the hunger artist down a couple of steps out of the cage, where on a small table a carefully chosen hospital meal was laid out. And at this moment the hunger artist always fought back. Of course, he still freely laid his bony arms in the helpful outstretched hands of the ladies bending over him, but he did not want to stand up. Why stop right now after forty days? He could have kept going for even longer, for an unlimited length of time. Why stop right now, when he was in his best form,

indeed, not yet even in his best fasting form? Why did
people want to rob him of the fame of fasting longer, not
just so that he could become the greatest hunger artist
of all time, which he probably was already, but also so
that he could surpass himself in some unimaginable way,
for he felt there were no limits to his capacity for fasting.
Why did this crowd, which pretended to admire him so
much, have so little patience with him? If he kept going
and kept fasting longer, why would they not tolerate it?
Then, too, he was tired and felt good sitting in the straw.
Now he was supposed to stand up straight and tall and
go to eat, something which, when he just imagined it,
made him feel nauseous right away. With great difficulty
he repressed mentioning this only out of consideration
for the women. And he looked up into the eyes of these
women, apparently so friendly but in reality so cruel, and
shook his excessively heavy head on his feeble neck.

But then happened what always happened. The
impresario came and in silence—the music made talking impossible—raised his arms over the hunger artist,
as if inviting heaven to look upon its work here on the
straw, this unfortunate martyr, something the hunger
artist certainly was, only in a completely different sense,
then grabbed the hunger artist around his thin waist,
in the process wanting with his exaggerated caution to
make people believe that here he had to deal with something fragile, and handed him over—not without secretly
shaking him a little, so that the hunger artist's legs and
upper body swung back and forth uncontrollably—to the
women, who had in the meantime turned as pale as death.
At this point, the hunger artist endured everything. His
head lay on his chest—it was as if it had inexplicably rolled

around and just stopped there—his body was arched
back, his legs, in an impulse of self-preservation, pressed
themselves together at the knees, but scraped the ground,
as if they were not really on the floor but were looking
for the real ground, and the entire weight of his body,
admittedly very small, lay against one of the women, who
appealed for help with flustered breath, for she had not
imagined her post of honour would be like this, and then
stretched her neck as far as possible, to keep her face from
the least contact with the hunger artist, but then, when
she couldn't manage this and her more fortunate companion didn't come to her assistance but trembled and
remained content to hold in front of her the hunger artist's hand, that small bundle of knuckles, she broke into
tears, to the delighted laughter of the auditorium, and
had to be relieved by an attendant who had been standing
ready for some time. Then came the meal. The impresario
put a little food into mouth of the hunger artist, now half
unconscious, as if fainting, and kept up a cheerful patter
designed to divert attention away from the hunger artist's condition. Then a toast was proposed to the public,
which was supposedly whispered to the impresario by the
hunger artist, the orchestra confirmed everything with a
great fanfare, people dispersed, and no one had the right
to be dissatisfied with the event, no one except the hunger
artist—he was always the only one.

He lived this way, taking small regular breaks, for many
years, apparently in the spotlight, honoured by the world,
but for all that his mood was usually gloomy, and it kept
growing gloomier all the time, because no one understood
how to take him seriously. But how was he to find consolation? What was there left for him to wish for? And if

a good-natured man who felt sorry for him ever wanted to explain to him that his sadness probably came from his fasting, then it could happen that the hunger artist responded with an outburst of rage and began to shake the bars like an animal, frightening everyone. But the impresario had a way of punishing moments like this, something he was happy to use. He would make an apology for the hunger artist to the assembled public, conceding that the irritability had been provoked only by his fasting, something quite intelligible to well-fed people and capable of excusing the behaviour of the hunger artist without further explanation. From there he would move on to speak about the equally hard to understand claim of the hunger artist that he could go on fasting for much longer than he was doing. He would praise the lofty striving, the good will, and the great self-denial no doubt contained in this claim, but then would try to contradict it simply by producing photographs, which were also on sale, for in the pictures one could see the hunger artist on the fortieth day of his fast, in bed, almost dead from exhaustion. Although the hunger artist was very familiar with this perversion of the truth, it always strained his nerves again and was too much for him. What was a result of the premature ending of the fast people were now proposing as its cause! It was impossible to fight against this lack of understanding, against this world of misunderstanding. In good faith he always listened eagerly to the impresario at the bars of his cage, but each time, once the photographs came out, he would let go of the bars and, with a sigh, sink back into the straw, and a reassured public could come up again and view him.

When those who had witnessed such scenes thought

back on them a few years later, often they were unable to understand themselves. For in the meantime that change mentioned above had set it. It happened almost immediately. There may have been more profound reasons for it, but who bothered to discover what they were? At any rate, one day the pampered hunger artist saw himself abandoned by the crowd of pleasure seekers, who preferred to stream to other attractions. The impresario chased around half of Europe one more time with him, to see whether he could still re-discover the old interest here and there. It was all futile. It was as if a secret agreement against the fasting performances had developed everywhere. Naturally, it couldn't really have happened all at once, and people later remembered some things which in the days of intoxicating success they hadn't paid sufficient attention to, some inadequately suppressed indications, but now it was too late to do anything to counter them. Of course, it was certain that the popularity of fasting would return once more someday, but for those now alive that was no consolation. What was the hunger artist to do now? A man whom thousands of people had cheered on could not display himself in show booths at small fun fairs. The hunger artist was not only too old to take up a different profession, but was fanatically devoted to fasting more than anything else. So he said farewell to the impresario, an incomparable companion on his life's road, and let himself be hired by a large circus. In order to spare his own feelings, he didn't even look at the terms of his contract at all.

A large circus with its huge number of men, animals, and gimmicks, which are constantly being let go and replenished, can use anyone at any time, even a hunger artist, provided, of course, his demands are modest. Moreover, in this particular case it was not only the hunger artist himself who was engaged, but also his old and famous name. In fact, given the characteristic nature of his art, which was not diminished by his advancing age, one could never claim that a worn out artist, who no longer stood at the pinnacle of his ability, wanted to escape to a quiet position in the circus. On the contrary, the hunger artist declared that he could fast just as well as in earlier times—something that was entirely credible. Indeed, he even affirmed that if people would let him do what he wanted—and he was promised this without further ado— he would really now legitimately amaze the world for the first time, an assertion which, however, given the mood of the time, which the hunger artist in his enthusiasm easily overlooked, only brought smiles from the experts.

However, basically the hunger artist had not forgotten his sense of the way things really were, and he took it as self-evident that people would not set him and his cage up as the star attraction somewhere in the middle of the arena, but would move him outside in some other readily accessible spot near the animal stalls. Huge brightly painted signs surrounded the cage and announced what there was to look at there. During the intervals in the main performance, when the general public pushed out towards the menagerie in order to see the animals, they could hardly avoid moving past the hunger artist and stopping there a moment. They would perhaps have remained with him longer, if those pushing up behind them in the narrow passage way, who did not understand this pause on the way to the animal stalls they wanted to see, had not made a longer peaceful observation impossible. This was also the reason why the hunger artist began to tremble at these visiting hours, which he naturally used to long for as the main purpose of his life. In the early days he could hardly wait for the pauses in the performances. He had looked forward with delight to the crowd pouring around him, until he became convinced only too quickly—and even the most stubborn, almost deliberate self-deception could not hold out against the experience—that, judging by their intentions, most of these people were, again and again without exception, only visiting the menagerie. And this view from a distance still remained his most beautiful moment. For when they had come right up to him, he immediately got an earful from the shouting of the two steadily increasing groups, the ones who wanted to take their time looking at the hunger artist, not with any understanding but on a whim or from mere defiance—for him these ones were soon the more painful—and a second group of people whose only demand was to go straight to the animal stalls.

Once the large crowds had passed, the late comers would arrive, and although there was nothing preventing these people any more from sticking around for as long as they wanted, they rushed past with long strides, almost without a sideways glance, to get to the animals in time. And it was an all-too-rare stroke of luck when the father of a family came by with his children, pointed his finger at the hunger artist, gave a detailed explanation about what was going on here, and talked of earlier years, when he had been present at similar but incomparably more magnificent performances, and then the children, because they had been inadequately prepared at school and in life, always stood around still uncomprehendingly. What was fasting to them? But nonetheless the brightness of the look in their searching eyes revealed something of new and more gracious times coming. Perhaps, the hunger artist said to himself sometimes, everything would be a little better if his location were not quite so near the animal stalls. That way it would be easy for people to make their choice, to say nothing of the fact that he was very upset and constantly depressed by the stink from the stalls, the animals' commotion at night, the pieces of raw meat dragged past him for the carnivorous beasts, and the roars at feeding time. But he did not dare to approach the administration about it. In any case, he had the animals to thank for the crowds of visitors among whom, here and there, there could be one destined for him. And who knew where they would hide him if he wished to remind them of his existence and, along with that, of the fact that, strictly speaking, he was only an obstacle on the way to the menagerie.

A small obstacle, at any rate, a constantly diminishing obstacle. People got used to the strange notion that in these times they would want to pay attention to a hunger artist, and with this habitual awareness the judgment on him was pronounced. He might fast as well as he could— and he did—but nothing could save him any more. People went straight past him. Try to explain the art of fasting to anyone! If someone doesn't feel it, then he cannot be made to understand it. The beautiful signs became dirty and illegible. People tore them down, and no one thought of replacing them. The small table with the number of days the fasting had lasted, which early on had been carefully renewed every day, remained unchanged for a long time, for after the first weeks the staff grew tired of even this small task. And so the hunger artist kept fasting on and on, as he once had dreamed about in earlier times, and he had no difficulty succeeding in achieving what he had predicted back then, but no one was counting the days—no one, not even the hunger artist himself, knew how great his achievement was by this point, and his heart grew heavy. And when once in a while a person strolling past stood there making fun of the old number and talking of a swindle, that was in a sense the stupidest lie which indifference and innate maliciousness could invent, for the hunger artist was not being deceptive—he was working honestly—but the world was cheating him of his reward.

Many days went by once more, and this, too, came to an end. Finally the cage caught the attention of a supervisor, and he asked the attendant why they had left this perfectly useful cage standing here unused with rotting straw inside. Nobody knew, until one man, with the help of the table with the number on it, remembered the hunger artist. They pushed the straw around with a pole and found the hunger artist in there. "Are you still fasting?" the supervisor asked. "When are you finally going to stop?" "Forgive me everything," whispered the hunger artist. Only the supervisor, who was pressing his ear up against the cage, understood him. "Certainly," said the supervisor, tapping his forehead with his finger in order to indicate to the spectators the state the hunger artist was in, "we forgive you." "I always wanted you to admire my fasting," said the hunger artist. "But we do admire it," said the supervisor obligingly. "But you shouldn't admire it," said the hunger artist. "Well then, we don't admire it," said the supervisor, "but why shouldn't we admire it?"

"Because I had to fast. I can't do anything else," said the hunger artist. "Just look at you," said the supervisor, "why can't you do anything else?" "Because," said the hunger artist, lifting his head a little and, with his lips pursed as if for a kiss, speaking right into the supervisor's ear so that he wouldn't miss anything, "because I couldn't find a food which I enjoyed. If had found that, believe me, I would not have made a spectacle of myself and would have eaten to my heart's content, like you and everyone else." Those were his last words, but in his failing eyes there was the firm, if no longer proud, conviction that he was continuing to fast.

"All right, tidy this up now," said the supervisor. And they buried the hunger artist along with the straw. But in his cage they put a young panther. Even for a person with the dullest mind it was clearly refreshing to see this wild animal throwing itself around in this cage, which had been dreary for such a long time. It lacked nothing. Without thinking about it for any length of time, the guards brought the animal food. It enjoyed the taste and never seemed to miss its freedom. This noble body, equipped with everything necessary, almost to the point of bursting, also appeared to carry freedom around with it. That seem to be located somewhere or other in its teeth, and its joy in living came with such strong passion from its throat that it was not easy for spectators to keep watching. But they controlled themselves, kept pressing around the cage, and had no desire to move on.

Translated by Ian Johnston

The Man without Qualities
Robert Musil

A MAN WITHOUT QUALITIES
CONSISTS OF QUALITIES WITHOUT A MAN.

Ulrich did not get there that evening. After Director
Fischel had hurried away, leaving him alone, he again
became preoccupied with the question of his youth, wondering why all figurative and (in the higher sense of the
word) untrue utterances were so uncannily favored by the
world. "One always gets one step further ahead precisely

ROBERT MUSIL (born in Klagenfurt, Carinthia, in 1880–
died in exile in Geneva in 1942) could have pursued a career in
science, but like the prominent Viennese writers around 1900 he
believed that literature provided the best future. His first book,
The Confusions of Young Törless, brought him instant acclaim, but
as a perfectionist he wrote slowly and never earned a living from
his writings. In 1938 he fled to Switzerland to escape the German annexation of Austria. He completed a number of masterful
shorter narrative texts, *Five Women* and *Posthumous Papers of a
Living Author,* but devoted most of his mature life to his magnum
opus, *The Man without Qualities,* supported by his publisher and
friends. However, he died of a stroke before he could complete it.
Nevertheless, critics praise this work as one of the greatest novels
in the German language.

when one is lying," he thought. "I ought to have told him
that as well."

Ulrich was a passionate man; but "passion" here should
not be taken as meaning the collective of what are called
"the passions." There must have been something that had
time and again driven him into the latter, and this was
perhaps passion, but in the actual state of excitement and
of excited actions his attitude was at once passionate and
detached. He had gone in for more or less everything there
was and felt that even now he might at any time plunge
into something that need not mean anything at all to him
if only it happened to stimulate his urge for action. So he
could with little exaggeration say of his life that everything in it had fulfilled itself as if it all belonged together
more than it belonged to him. He had always been "in for
a penny, in for a pound," whether in contest or in love.
And so he more or less had to believe that the personal
qualities he had gained in this way belonged more to each
other than to him, indeed that everyone of them, when
he examined it closely, was no more intimately bound up
with him than with other people who might also happen
to possess it.

But undoubtedly one was nevertheless conditioned by
them and consisted of them, even if one was not identical
with them, and so sometimes when at rest one seemed to
oneself precisely as much a stranger as when in motion.
If Ulrich had been asked to say what he was really like,
he would have been at a loss; for like many people he had
never tested himself otherwise than in the performance
of a task and in his relation to it. His self-confidence had
not been damaged, nor was it coddled and vain, and it felt

no need for that kind of overhauling and greasing that is called examining one's conscience. Was he a strong personality? He didn't know; on this score he was perhaps fatefully mistaken. But he was certainly a man who had always had confidence in his strength. Even now he had no doubt that this difference between having one's own experiences and qualities and remaining a stranger to them was only a difference in attitude, in a certain sense an act of will or a matter of living on a chosen latitude between generality and individuality. To put it quite simply, one's attitude to the things that happen to one and that one does can be either more general or more personal. One can feel a blow not only as pain but as an affront, which will intensify it intolerably; but one can also take it in a sporting spirit, as an obstacle that must not be allowed either to intimidate one or get one into a state of blind rage, and then it not infrequently happens that one does not notice it at all. In this second case, however, nothing has happened but that one has sorted it into its place in a larger complex, namely that of combat, as a result of which its nature proves to be dependent on the task that it has to fulfill. And precisely this phenomenon—that an experience gets its significance, even its content, only from its position, in a chain of logically consistent actions—is apparent in everyone who regards experience not merely as something personal but as a challenge to his spiritual strength. He too will then experience his actions more faintly. But, oddly enough, what is considered superior intelligence in boxing is called cold and callous as soon as it occurs, from a liking for an intellectual attitude to life, in people who cannot box. There are in fact also all sorts of other distinctions in use by the aid of which it is possible to adopt or insist on a general or a personal attitude, according to the situation. If a murderer proceeds in a matter-of-fact and efficient manner, it will be interpreted as particular brutality. A professor who goes on working out a problem in his wife's arms will be reproached with being a dry-as-dust pedant. A politician who climbs high over the bodies of the slain is described as vile or great according to the degree of his success. Of soldiers, executioners, and surgeons, on the other hand, precisely the same cold-bloodedness is demanded as is condemned in others. It is not necessary to go into the moral of these examples any further in order to be struck by the uncertainty leading, in every case, to a compromise between objectively correct and personally correct conduct.

This uncertainty formed a wide background to Ulrich's personal problem. In earlier times one could be an individual with a better conscience than one can today. People used to be like the stalks of corn in the field. They were probably more violently flung to and fro by God, hail, fire, pestilence, and war than they are today, but it was collectively, in terms of towns, of countrysides, the field as a whole; and whatever was left to the individual stalk in the way of personal movement was something that could be answered for and was clearly defined. Today, on the other hand, responsibility's point of gravity lies not in the individual but in the relations between things. Has one not noticed that experiences have made themselves independent of man? They have gone on to the stage, into books, into the reports of scientific institutions and expeditions, into communities based on religious or other conviction, which develop certain kinds of experience at the cost of all the others as in a social experiment; and in so far as experiences are not merely to be found in work, they are simply in the air. Who today can still say that his anger is really his own anger, with so many people butting in and knowing so much more about it than he does? There has arisen a world of qualities without a man to them, of experiences without anyone to experience them, and it almost looks as though under ideal conditions man would no longer experience anything at all privately and the comforting weight of personal responsibility would dissolve into a system of formulae for potential meanings. It is probable that the dissolution of the anthropocentric attitude (an attitude that, after so long seeing man as the center of the universe, has been dissolving for some centuries now) has finally begun to affect the personality itself; for the belief that the most important thing about experience is the experiencing of it, and about deeds the doing of them, is beginning to strike most people as naive. Doubtless there are still people who experience things quite personally, saying "we were at So-and-So's yesterday" or, "we'll do this or that today" and enjoying it without its needing to have any further content or significance. They like everything that their fingers touch, and are persons as purely private as is possible. The world becomes a private world as soon as it comes into contact with them, and shines like a rainbow. Perhaps they are very happy; but this kind of people now usually appears absurd to the others, although it is as yet by no means established why.

And all at once, in the midst of these reflections, Ulrich

had to confess to himself, smiling, that for all this he was, after all, a "character," even without having one.

A MAN WITH ALL THE QUALITIES, BUT THEY ARE A MATTER OF INDIFFERENCE TO HIM. A MASTERMIND IS ARRESTED, AND THE COLLATERAL CAMPAIGN GETS ITS HONORARY SECRETARY.

It is not difficult to give a description of this thirty-two-year-old man, Ulrich, in general outline, even though all he knew about himself was that he was as far from all the qualities as he was near to them, and that all of them, whether they had become his own or not, in some strange way were equally a matter of indifference to him. Associated with his intellectual suppleness, which was based simply on a great variety of gifts, there was, in him, a certain bellicosity too. He was of a masculine turn of mind. He was not sensitive where other people were concerned and rarely tried to get inside their minds, except when he wanted to understand them for his own ends. He had no respect for rights when he did not respect those whose rights they were, and that happened rarely. For with the passing of time he had developed a certain readiness to adopt negative attitudes, a flexible dialectic of feeling that was inclined to tempt him into discovering defects in what was generally approved of and defending what was considered beyond the pale, and into rejecting obligations with an irritation arising out of a determination to create obligations of his own. In spite of this determination, however, with certain exceptions that he considered his due he simply left his moral conduct to that chivalrous

code that is the guide of more or less all men in bourgeois
society so long as they are living in settled circumstances;
and in this manner, with all the arrogance, ruthlessness
and nonchalance of a man who is conscious of his own
vocation, he led the life of another person who made more
or less ordinary, utilitarian and social use of his tastes and
abilities. It was natural to him to regard himself—quite
without vanity—as the instrument of a not unimportant
purpose of which he felt certain he would, all in good time,
discover more; and even now, in this newly begun year of
groping unrest, after he had realized how his life had been
drifting, the feeling of being on the way somewhere soon
returned and he made no particular effort with his plans.
It is not altogether easy to recognize the driving passion
in a temperament like this, which has been ambiguously
shaped by natural talents and by circumstances, so long as
its fate has not been laid bare by any really hard counter-
pressure. But the main thing is that it still lacks some
factor unknown such as would make a decision possible.
Ulrich was a man whom something compelled to live
against his own grain, although he seemed to let himself
float along without any constraint.

The comparison of the world with a laboratory reminded
him of an old idea of his. Formerly he had thought of the
kind of life that would appeal to him as a large experimen-
tal station, where the best ways of living as a human being
would be tried out and new ones discovered. The fact that
this whole complex of laboratories worked more or less
haphazardly, without any directors or theoreticians, was
another matter. It might even be said that he himself had
wanted to become something like a dominant spirit and

mastermind. And who, after all, would not? It is so natural for the mind to be considered the highest of all things, ruling over all things. That is what we are taught. All and sundry adorn themselves with mind, use it as trimming wherever possible. Mind and spirit, when in combination with something else, are the most widespread thing there is. There is a masculine mind, a cultured mind, the greatest living mind, the spirit of loyalty, the spirit of love, "keeping up the spirit" of this cause or that, "acting in the spirit of our movement" and so forth. How solid and unimpeachable it sounds, right down to the lowest levels! Everything else, the everyday crime or bustling greed for gain, appears by contrast as that which is never admitted, the dirt that God removes from under His toenails.

But when the spirit stands alone, a naked noun, bare as a ghost to whom one would like to lend a sheet—what then? One can read the poets, study the philosophers, buy pictures and have discussions all night long. But is it spirit that one gains by doing so? Assuming one does gain it—does one then possess it? This something called spirit, so firmly bound up with the form in which it happens to manifest itself, passes through the person who wants to receive and harbor it, leaving nothing behind but a slight tremor. What are we to do with all this spirit? It is continually being produced on masses of paper, stone and canvas, in downright astronomical quantities, and is being as ceaselessly ingested and consumed with a gigantic expenditure of nervous energy. But what happens to it then? Does it vanish like a mirage? Does it dissolve into particles? Is it an exception to the natural law of conservation? The dust particles sinking down into us, slowly settling, are in no relation to all the trouble involved. Where has it gone? Where, what, is it? Perhaps, if one knew more about it, there would be an awkward silence round this noun "spirit" . . .

Evening had come. Buildings, as though broken out of their setting in space, asphalt, steel rails—all this formed the now cooling shell of the city. In this maternal shell, filled with childlike, joyful, angry human movement, every drip begins as a droplet, frothing and splashing, begins with a tiny explosion and is caught up by the walls and cooled off, becoming milder, more quiescent, cling-ing tenderly to the inner wall of the mother shell and finally solidifying, setting fast there as a little grain of substance.

"Why," Ulrich suddenly thought, "why didn't I become a pilgrim?" A pure, unconditional way of living, hecti-cally fresh as very clear air, spread out before his mind's eye. Anyone who did not want to accept life as it was should at least reject it as the saints did; and yet it was simply impossible to consider that seriously. Nor could he become a traveler and adventurer, although that life might well have a touch of perpetual honeymoon, and he felt the impulse to it in his limbs as in his tempera-ment. He had not been capable of becoming either a poet or one of those disappointed people who believed only in money and power, although he had had the makings of either, as of everything. He forgot his age, imagining he was twenty. Nevertheless, it had been just as finally decided within him even then that he could not become any of these things. There was something attracting him to everything there was, and something stronger that

would not let him get to it. Why did he live so vaguely and
undecidedly? Undoubtedly—he said to himself—what
kept him, as under a spell, in this aloof and anonymous
form of existence was nothing but the compulsion to that
loosing and binding of the world that is known by a word
one does not like to encounter alone: spirit.

And though he himself did not know why, Ulrich
suddenly felt sad and thought: "It's simply that I'm not
fond of myself." In the frozen, petrified body of the town,
in its innermost depths, he felt his own heart beating.
There was something in him that had never wanted to
stay anywhere, but had groped its way along the walls
of the world, thinking. There are still millions of other
walls. It was this ridiculous drop of Self, slowly growing cold, that did not want to give up its fire, the tiny
red-hot core within it. The mind has learned that beauty
can make things good, bad, stupid or enchanting. The
mind dissects and analyzes a sheep and a penitent sinner
and finds humility and patience in both. It investigates
a substance and observes that in large quantities it is a
poison, in smaller quantities a stimulant. It knows that
the mucous membrane of the lips is related to the mucous
membrane of the intestine, but knows too that the humility of those lips is related to the humility of all that is
saintly. It mixes things up, unravels them again and forms
new combinations. Good and evil, above and below, are
for it not relative ideas tinged with skepticism, but terms
of a function, values dependent on the context in which
they appear. It has learned from the centuries that vices
may turn into virtues and virtues into vices, and actually
regards it as sheer clumsiness if one does not in one life-

time succeed in turning a criminal into a useful citizen.
It does not recognize anything as in itself permissible or
impermissible, for anything may have a quality by which
it some day becomes part of a great new relationship. It
secretly has a mortal hatred of everything that behaves
as though it were established once and for all, the great
ideals and laws and their little fossilized imprint, the
hedged-in character. It regards nothing as firmly established, neither any personality nor any order of things or
ideas. Because our knowledge may change with every day,
it believes in no ties, and everything possesses the value
that it has only until the next act of creation, as a face to
which one is speaking changes even while the words are
being spoken.

For the spirit of man is the great opportunist, but cannot
itself be seized hold of anywhere; and one might almost
believe that nothing is brought about by its influence but
decay. All progress means a gain in each particular case,
but also a severance from the wholeness of things; and
this means an increase in power, which leads to a progres-
sive increase in powerlessness, and there is no leaving off.
Ulrich was reminded of the almost hourly growing body
of facts and discoveries out of which the mind has to peer
forth today if it wants to scrutinize any question closely.
This body grows away from the inner being. Although
there are countless views, opinions, and classificatory
ideas from all latitudes and ages, from all sorts of sound
and sick brains, waking and dreaming brains, lacing it
like thousands of sensitive little nerve skeins, yet there is
no central point where they all unite. Man feels he is dan-
gerously near the stage where he will suffer the same fate

as those gigantic primeval animals that perished because of their size. But he can't leave off.

And this brought Ulrich back to that rather dubious notion in which he had long believed and which he had even now not quite rooted out of himself: that the world would be best governed by a senate of highly evolved men possessing great knowledge. It is, after all, very natural to think that man who lets himself be treated by professionally qualified doctors when he is ill, and not by shepherd lads, has no reason when in good health to let himself be treated, as he actually does in his public affairs, by windbags whose qualifications are no better than those of shepherd lads. And that is why young people who have the essentials of life at heart start out by thinking everything in the world that is neither true nor good nor beautiful— such as for instance the inland revenue department or, to keep to the point, a parliamentary debate—unimportant. At least, that is the way they used to think in those days. Nowadays, thanks to education in politics and economics, they are said to be different. But even then, when one grew older—and on longer acquaintance with the smoking chamber of the mind, where the world cures the bacon of its business—one learned to adapt oneself to reality; and the final condition of the qualified intellectual was approximately this—that he restricted himself to his "subject" and spent the rest of his life in the conviction that although perhaps everything ought to be different, there was certainly no point in thinking about it. This is a pretty fair picture of the inner equilibrium of the people who follow intellectual pursuits. And all at once the whole thing presented itself to Ulrich comically, in the question whether in the end, since there was certainly plenty of mind and spirit knocking about, all that was wrong was that the spirit was mere spirit and the mind had no mind?

He felt like laughing at that. After all, he himself was one of those specialists who renounced all else. But disappointed ambition, still alive, went through him like a sword. In this moment two Ulrichs walked side by side.

The one looked around, smiling, and thought: "So that's where I once wanted to play a part, against such a stage decor. One day I woke up, not snug as in mother's little basket, but with the firm conviction that I must accomplish something. I was given my cues, and I felt they did not concern me. Everything was filled with my own intentions and expectations, as though with flickering stagefright. But in the meantime the stage revolved without my noticing it, I got a bit further on my way, and now perhaps I am already standing at the exit. In next to no time it will have turned me right out, and all I shall have spoken of my great part will be: 'The horses are saddled.' The devil take the lot of you!"

But while the one walked through the floating evening, smiling at these thoughts, the other had his fists clenched in pain and anger. He was the less visible of the two. And what he was thinking of was how to find a magic formula, a lever that one might be able to get a hold of, the real mind of the mind, the missing, perhaps very small, bit that would close the broken circle. This second Ulrich had no words at his disposal. Words leap like monkeys from tree to tree; but in the dark realm where a man is rooted he lacks their friendly mediation. The ground streamed away under his feet. He could hardly open his eyes. Can a feeling blow like a storm and yet not be a stormy feeling at all? If one speaks of a storm of emotion, one means the kind in which man's bark groans and man's branches fly as though they were about to break. But this was a storm with a quite calm surface. It was almost, but not quite, a state of conversion, of reversion. There was no shift in the expression of the face, but inwardly no atom seemed to remain in its place. Ulrich's senses were unclouded, and yet each person he went past was perceived differently from usual by his eye, each sound differently by his ear. It would be wrong to say: more sharply; nor was it more deeply either, nor more softly, more naturally, or more unnaturally. Ulrich could not say anything at all, but at this moment he thought of the strange experience that "spirit" is as of a beloved by whom one has been deceived all one's life long, without loving her any the less for that; and this united him with everything that came his way. For when one loves, everything is love, even when it is pain and loathing. The little twig on the tree and the pale windowpane in the evening light became an experience sunk deep in his own essential nature, an experience that could scarcely be expressed in words. Things seemed not to be of wood and stone; it was as if their fabric were a grand and infinitely delicate immorality, which, in the moment when it came into contact with him, turned into a shock of deep moral emotion.

That lasted as long as a smile. And Ulrich was just thinking: "Now for once I'll stay put where it has swept me" when, as bad luck would have it, this tension crashed against an obstacle.

What happened now actually originated in an utterly
different world from that in which Ulrich had just been
experiencing trees and stones as a sensitive extension of
his own body.

For a working-class paper had, as Count Leinsdorf
would have put it, poured destructive venom on the
Great Idea, asserting that it was merely a new sensation
for the ruling class, following up the last sexual murder ;
and this inflammatory talk had affected a worthy laborer
who had drunk a little too much. He brushed against two
respectable citizens who were feeling contented with their
day's business and who, secure in the consciousness that
right and proper opinions could be aired at any time, were
somewhat loudly expressing their approval of the patriotic
Campaign, of which they had read in their paper. There
was an exchange of "words." And because the proximity of
a policeman was as encouraging to the loyal citizens as it
was provoking to the attacker, the scene became increasingly impassioned. The policeman at first watched it over
his shoulder, and then turned round, and gradually drew
closer; he was present as an observer, like a protruding arm
of the iron machinery of the State, complete with buttons
and other metal parts. The fact is, living permanently in
a well-ordered State has an out-and-out spectral aspect:
one cannot step into the street or drink a glass of water or
get into a tram without touching the perfectly balanced
levers of a gigantic apparatus of laws and relations, setting them in motion or letting them maintain one in the
peace and quiet of one's existence. One knows hardly any
of these levers, which extend deep into the inner work-
ings and on the other side are lost in a network the entire

constitution of which has never been disentangled by any living being. Hence one denies their existence, just as the common man denies the existence of the air, insisting that it is mere emptiness; but it seems that precisely this is what lends life a certain spectral quality—the fact that everything that is denied reality, everything that is colorless, odorless, tasteless, imponderable and nonmoral, like water, air, space, money, and the passing of time, is in reality what is most important. Man is at times seized with panic as in the helplessness of dream, by a gale of movement, wildly lashing out like an animal that has got into the incomprehensible mechanism of a net. Such was the effect the policeman's buttons had on the laborer, and it was at this moment that the officer of the law, feeling that he was not being paid due respect, proceeded to make the arrest.

This did not take place without resistance and repeated manifestation of a seditious attitude. The sensation so caused was flattering to the drunk man, and a previously concealed total dislike of his fellow creatures now broke out into the open. A passionate struggle for self-assertion began. A higher sense of his own ego came into conflict with an uncanny feeling of not being quite firmly fixed in his own skin. And the world too was not quite solid; it was an unsteady mist, continually becoming distorted and changing its shape. Buildings stood crookedly broken out of space. Between them were ridiculous, swarming, yet all kindred silly fools, the people. "I am called to put things straight here," felt the man in this extraordinary state of drunkenness. The whole scene was filled with something flickering. Some piece of what was happening came clearly toward him like a few yards of road, but then the walls revolved again. His eyes felt as if they were standing out of his head on long stalks, while the soles of his feet clung to the ground. A strange and wonderful outpouring came from his mouth; out of his innermost being came words of which there was no telling how they had first got in there, and possibly they were words of abuse. It wasn't so easy to be sure. The outside and inside of things collapsed upon each other. This anger was no inner anger, but only the bodily shell of anger worked up to fury, and a policeman's face came very slowly closer to a clenched fist, and then it was bleeding.

But the policeman had trebled meanwhile. As the policemen came hurrying up, a crowd gathered. The drunk man had thrown himself on the ground and was resisting arrest. Then Ulrich committed an imprudence. He had heard the words "insulting His Majesty" and now remarked that in his present condition the man was not capable of insulting anyone, and that he ought to be sent home to sleep it off. He did not think anything of it, but he had met with the wrong people. The man shouted that for all he cared Ulrich and His Majesty could both go and be . . . And a policeman, who obviously attributed the blame for this relapse to the interference, barked at Ulrich to move on. Now, as it happened, Ulrich was not accustomed to regard the State as anything but a hotel in which one was entitled to civility and service, and he objected to the tone in which he had been addressed. This quite unexpectedly caused the police to see that one drunk was not sufficient reason for the presence of three officers of the law, whereupon they took Ulrich in charge as well.

The hand of a uniformed man clutched his arm. His arm was a good deal stronger than this offensive clutch, but he could not very well break out of it unless he wanted to let himself in for a hopeless boxing match with the armed minions of the State. So there was nothing else for him to do but to utter a polite request that he might be allowed to come along voluntarily. The station was in the district headquarters building. When he came in, the floor and walls reminded Ulrich of barracks. They showed signs of the same somber battle between the dirt that was being continually carried in and the crude detergents used against it. The next thing he noticed was the appointed symbol of civil authority: two writing desks, each topped by a little ornamental balustrade from which several little columns were missing, hardly more than a crate for writing on, the cloth inlay torn and scorched, the whole thing resting on very low ball-feet and showing the last chipped traces of the yellow-brown varnish with which it had once been coated, away back in the days of the Emperor Ferdinand. The third thing was that the room was permeated by the dense feeling that this was a place where one had to wait without asking questions. Ulrich's own policeman, after reporting the grounds for arrest, stood beside him like a pillar. Ulrich tried to give some explanation at once. The sergeant in control of this fortress raised an eye from a form that he had been filling in when prisoners and escort came in, and surveyed Ulrich; the eye then sank again, and he continued filling in the form. Ulrich got a whiff of infinity. Then the sergeant pushed the form aside, took a book from the shelf, made an entry, sprinkled sand on it, put the book back, took another, made an entry,

sprinkled sand, pulled a file out of a bundle of similar
files and continued his activities with this. Ulrich got the
feeling that now a second infinity was unfolding, in the
course of which the constellations went on their predestined cycles, without his being in the world at all.

From this office an open door led into a corridor with
the cells on each side. That was where Ulrich's protege had
been taken immediately, and since there was no further
sound from him, it seemed likely that the blessing of sleep
had descended upon him. But there was also the feeling
of uncanny other things going on. The corridor with the
cells along it must have a second entrance. Ulrich repeat-
edly heard heavy-footed comings and goings, slamming
of doors, lowered voices. And all at once, when some other
person was brought in, one of these voices rose and Ulrich
heard it implore in despairing tones: "If you have a spark
of human feeling, don't arrest me!" The voice broke, and
there was something oddly out-of-place, almost laughable,
in this appeal to a functionary to have feelings, since func-
tions are after all only carried out in a matter-of-fact way.
The sergeant raised his head for a moment, without quite
withdrawing his attention from his file. Ulrich heard the
violent shuffling of many feet, the bodies of which were
evidently mutely pushing a resistant body. Then came the
sound of two feet alone, stumbling as though after a push.
A door slammed shut, a bolt clicked, the uniformed man
at the writing desk bent his head again, and in the air lay
the silence of a full stop that has been set at the right place
at the end of a sentence.

But Ulrich seemed to have been mistaken in his
assumption that as far as the cosmos of the police was

concerned he was not yet created. For the next time the sergeant raised his head he looked at him and the lines he had written last remained moist and glimmering, without being sprinkled with sand, and Ulrich—or rather, the case he was—all at once turned out to have been in official existence for some time. Name? Age? Occupation? Address? . . . Ulrich was being questioned.

He felt as though he had got caught up in a machine, which was splitting him up into impersonal, general component parts even before there was any mention of his guilt or innocence. His name—those two words that are conceptually the poorest, but emotionally the richest in the language—here counted for nothing. His work, which had brought him honor in the scientific world (usually considered so solid), did not exist for this world here; he was not asked about it even once. His face counted only from the point of view of "description." He had the feeling that he had never before thought about the fact that his eyes were gray eyes, belonging to one of the four officially recognized kinds of eyes in existence of which there were millions of specimens. His hair was fair, his build tall, his face oval, and his special peculiarities were none, although he himself was of a different opinion on this score. To his own way of feeling he was tall, his shoulders were broad, his chest expanded like a filled sail from the mast, and the joints of his body fastened his muscles off like small links of steel whenever he was angry or quarrelsome or, for instance, had Bonadea clinging to him. On the other hand, he was slim, lightly built, dark, and soft as a jellyfish floating in water whenever he was reading a book that moved him or was touched by a breath of that great and homeless love whose presence in the world he had never been able to fathom. And so even at this moment he could also appreciate the statistical disenchantment of his person, and the methods of measurement and description applied to him by the police officer aroused his enthusiasm as much as might a love poem invented by Satan. The most wonderful thing about it was that the police could not only dismantle a human being in this way, so that nothing remained of him, but that they would also put him together again out of these trifling components, unmistakably himself, and recognize him by them. All that is needed for this achievement is the addition of something imponderable, which they call "suspicion."

Ulrich all at once realized that it was only with the coolest of intelligence that he would be able to extricate himself from this situation into which his foolhardiness had got him. The questioning went on. He wondered what effect it would have if, when asked for his address, he were to answer: "My address is that of a person I do not know." Or if, in answer to the question why he had done what he had done, he were to answer that he always did something different from what he really cared about. But in outward reality he sedately named street and house number and tried to invent an extenuatory account of his behavior. The inner authority of the mind was meanwhile most distressingly helpless in the face of the external authority of the police sergeant. At last, however, he glimpsed a possibility of saving the situation. Although, when he was asked his occupation and made the statement "independent" (he could not have brought himself

to say he was "engaged in independent research") the
gaze he felt fixed on him was still of exactly the sort that
might have been expected if he had said "of no settled
abode" when his father's status was inquired into and it
appeared that he was a member of the Upper House, the
gaze underwent a transformation. It was still mistrustful,
but something about it at once gave Ulrich a feeling such
as a man tossed to and fro by the ocean waves might have
when his big toe scrapes on solid ground.

With rapidly awakening presence of mind he turned
this to account. He instantly modified everything he had
so far admitted; he confronted this authority, these ears
that had heard it all in their capacity as ears under official
oath, with the insistent request that he should be inter-
rogated by the superintendent himself; and, when this
merely caused a smile, he lied—with an utterly natural
air, quite casually, and prepared to go back on the assertion immediately in the event of its being knotted into
the noose of a demand for precise details—saying that
he was a friend of Count Leinsdorf's and secretary to the
great patriotic Campaign of which everyone had doubtless read in the newspapers. He at once observed that
this produced the graver state of thoughtfulness as to his
person that had up to now been denied him, and he held
on to his advantage.

The result was that the sergeant eyed him wrathfully,
for he did not want to take the responsibility either of
detaining this catch any longer or of letting it go; and
because at this hour there was no higher official in the
building, he resorted to a way out that was a handsome
testimonial to the fact that he, a simple sergeant, had

learned something of the way in which his superiors handled awkward cases. He put on an important air and expressed grave surmises as to how Ulrich seemed to be not only guilty of having insulted an officer of the law and of having interfered with the execution of his duty, but, worse still, considering the position he claimed to hold, also came under suspicion of being involved in obscure and perhaps political machinations, for which reason he must take the consequences of being handed over to the political department at police headquarters.

So a few minutes later Ulrich was driving through the night in a cab that he had been permitted to take, at his side a plainclothes man who was little disposed to conversation. As they approached headquarters, Ulrich saw the windows on the first floor festively illumined, for there was an important conference still going on at this late hour in the office of the President of Police himself. The building was far from being a dim and gloomy hole; it quite resembled a ministry. He began to breathe more familiar air. He soon noticed, too, that the officer on night duty, to whom he was brought, was quick to see the foolishness committed by the exasperated peripheral arm in arresting him. Nevertheless, it seemed utterly inadvisable to release from the clutches of the law anyone who had been so reckless as to run into them of his own accord. The officer here at headquarters also wore an iron machine in his face and assured the prisoner that his rashness made it appear extremely difficult to warrant his release. Ulrich had already twice gone over everything that had such a favorable effect on the sergeant, but where this higher-ranking officer was concerned it was all in vain. He was beginning to give himself up for lost, when all at once a remarkable, almost happy change occurred in the expression of the man in whose hands his fate lay. He read the charge again carefully, asked Ulrich for his name once more, made sure of his address and then very civilly asked him to wait a moment, whereupon he left the room.

It was ten minutes before he returned, looking like a man who had recollected something pleasant, and with marked courtesy invited the prisoner to follow him. At the door of a room where light was burning, a story higher, he said no more than: "The President of Police wishes to speak to you personally," and the next moment Ulrich stood before a gentleman with the muttonchop whiskers that had lately become familiar to him, who had just come in from the conference room next door.

He was determined to explain his presence as a mistake on the part of the district station, and in a tone of gentle reproach. But the President anticipated him, greeting him with the words: "A misunderstanding, my dear Herr von ———, the Inspector has already told me all about it. All the same, we must impose a little penalty, for—" and with these words he looked at him roguishly (in so far as the word "roguish" can at all be applied to the most exalted of police officials), as though he wanted him to solve the riddle himself.

But Ulrich entirely failed to guess.

"His Highness!" the President helped him on. "His Highness Count Leinsdorf," he added, "just a few hours ago came to me, inquiring for you most anxiously."

Ulrich only half understood this.

"You are not in the directory, my dear Herr von ———,"

the President explained in a tone of jesting reproach, as though that were Ulrich's only offense.

Ulrich bowed, smiling formally.

"I gather that you must call upon His Highness tomorrow on a matter of great public importance, and I cannot take it upon myself to prevent you from doing so by incarcerating you." In this manner the master of the iron machine concluded his little joke.

It may be assumed that the President would also in any other case have considered the arrest wrongful and that the Inspector, who happened to recollect the connection in which Ulrich's name had come up for the first time in this building a few hours earlier, had represented the incident to the President in such a way that the President was bound to come to this conclusion: in other words, no one had arbitrarily interfered with the course of events. His Highness, by the way, never learned how it all came about. Ulrich felt obliged to call on him on the day after this evening of *lèse-majesté*, and on this occasion was at once appointed honorary secretary to the great patriotic Campaign. Count Leinsdorf, had he known how it all came about, would not have been able to say anything but that it was like a miracle.

Translated by Eithne Wilkins and Ernst Kaiser

The Red Cock

Elias Canetti

PETER LOCKED THE DOOR behind his brother. It was
secured by three complicated locks and thick, heavy iron
bolts. He rattled them: not a nail shook. The whole door
was like a single piece of steel; behind it he was truly at
home. The keys still fitted; the paint on the wood had
faded; it felt rough to the touch. The rust on the darkened
bolts was old and it was hard to make out what part of the
door had been repaired. Surely the caretaker had smashed

ELIAS CANETTI (born in Bulgaria in 1905–died in Zürich
in 1994), dramatist, essayist, and novelist, grew up multinational
and multilingual. He was raised in England, Austria, and Germany, and knew Bulgarian, German, English, Ladino, and
some French. He was educated in Austria, where he assimilated
into the life and the culture and became part of the Austrian
literary tradition. Canetti fled to England in 1938 to escape the
Nazi annexation of Austria, but the majority of his works deal
with Austrian themes, regardless of where he lived. The political demonstrations that he witnessed in Vienna in 1927 during
the July Revolt were incorporated into his only novel, *Auto da
Fé*, from which the selection here is taken. The novel portrays
the turn to evil of an individual and of a nation, leading to
the destruction of both. Along with many other distinctions
Canetti was awarded the Nobel Prize for Literature in 1981.

---

it, when he had broken into the flat. A kick of his and
the bolts had snapped like wood; the wretched liar, he
lied with his fists and feet; he had simply crashed into the
flat. Once upon a time came the first of the month and
brought no honorarium for Mr. Pfaff. "Something's happened to him!" he had roared, and hurled himself upstairs
to the source of his income; it had suddenly dried up. On
the way he had battered the stairs. The stone whimpered
under his booted fists. The tenants crept out of their
dens, all his subjects in the house, and held their noses.
"It stinks!" they complained. "Where?" he asked threat-
eningly. "Out of the library." "I can stink nothing!" He
couldn't even speak his native tongue. He had a thick nose
and gigantic nostrils, but his moustache was twisted and
reached up into his nostrils. So he could smell nothing
but pomade, and as for the corpse he never smelled that.
His moustache was as stiff as ice, every day he waxed it.
He had red pomade in a thousand different tubes. Under
the bed in his closet was a collection of salve jars, red of
every color, red here, red there, red overhead. His head,
yes, his head was Fiery Red.

Kien put out the light in the hall. He only had to press
a switch and it grew dark at once. Through cracks in the
floor a pale glimmer reached him from the study and
gently stroked his trousers. How many trousers had he
not seen! The peephole existed no longer. The ruffian had
broken it off. The wall was left desolate. Tomorrow a new
Pfaff would move in down below and wall up the gash.
If only it had been staunched at once! The napkin was
stiff with blood. The water in the basin was reddened by
a sea-battle off the canary islands. Why had they hidden

themselves under the bed? There was room enough on the wall. There were four cages ready. But they looked down haughtily on the small fry. The fleshpots were empty. Then came the quails and the children of Israel could eat. All the birds were killed. Little throats they had, under their yellow feathers. Who would think it, that powerful voice, and yet how get at their little throats! Once you grasp them, you press them, there's an end of the four part song, blood spurts in all directions, thick, warm blood, these birds live in a perpetual fever, hot blood, it Burns, my trousers Burn.

Kien wiped the blood and the glow off his trousers. Instead of going into his study, whence the light assaulted him, he went through the long dark corridor into the kitchen. On the table was a plate of bread. The chair in front of it was crooked as if someone had just been sitting on it. He pushed it away with hostility. He seized the soft, yellow brioches, they were the birds' corpses, and poured them into the bread bin. It looked like a crematorium. He hid it away in the kitchen cupboard. On the table the plate alone was left, shining and dazzlingly white, a cushion. On top of it lay a book—"The Trousers . . ." Therese had opened it. She had stopped at page 20. She was wearing gloves. "I read every page six times." She was trying to seduce him. He wanted nothing but a glass of water. She fetched it. "I'm going away for six months." "Excuse me, I can't have it!" "It is necessary." "I can't have it." "But I'm going just the same." "Then I'll lock the door of the flat?" "I have the key." "Where, excuse me?" "Here!" "And if a Fire should break out?"

Kien went to the sink and turned the tap on full. With

full force the stream shot into the heavy basin; it almost broke it. Soon it was full of water. The flood streamed over the kitchen floor and quenched every danger. He turned the tap off again. He slipped on the stone tiles. He slipped into the bedroom next door. It was empty. He smiled at it. In earlier times there had been a bed here and against the opposite wall a trunk. In the bed the blue virago had slept. She kept her weapons hidden in the trunk; skirts, skirts and yet more skirts. Daily she performed her devotions at the ironing board in the corner. The limp folds were laid out on the table; they arose resurrected in their strength. Later she moved in with him and brought the furniture with her. The walls went pale with joy. They have been white ever since. And what did Therese pile up against them? Sacks of flour, great sacks of flour! She was making the bedroom into her store cupboard against the lean years. Thighs hung down from the ceiling, smoked thighs. The floor was abristle with sugar loaves. Bread rolls tumbled against kegs of butter. Milk cans sucked close up to each other. The sacks of flour against the wall defended the town from hostile attack. There were things laid up here for all eternity. She let herself be locked in, unperturbed, and bragged of her keys. One day she opened the bedroom door. There was not a crumb left in the kitchen and what did she find in the bedroom? The flour bags were nothing but holes. Instead of hams, strings hung from the ceiling. The milk had all run out of the cans, and the sugar loaves were only blue paper. The floor had eaten up the bread and smeared the butter into its cracks. Who has done this? Who? Rats! Rats appear suddenly in houses where there were never any before, no one knows where they come from, but there they are, they eat up everything, kind blessed rats, and they leave nothing behind for hungry women but a pile of newspapers; there they lie, nothing else. They don't care for newspaper. Rats hate cellulose. They maneuver in the darkness all right, but they are not termites. Termites eat wood and books. The love riot among the termites. Fire in the Library.

As fast as his arm would obey him, Kien clutched for a paper. He did not have to stoop far. The pile reached above his knee. He pushed it violently aside. The floor in front of the window all the way across was taken up with papers; all the old papers for years had been piled up here. He leaned out of the window. In the courtyard below all was dark. From the stars light penetrated to him. But it was not enough to read the paper by. Perhaps he was holding it too far off. He approached it to his eyes, his nose touched the surface and sucked in the faint smell of oil, greedy and fearful. The paper trembled and crackled. The wind which swayed the paper came from his nostrils, and his nails clawed through it. But his eyes were in quest of a headline so big that it could be read. Once he could get a hold of it, he would read the whole paper by starlight. First of all he made a huge M. So murder was the subject. Immediately next to it there was indeed a U. The headline, coarse and black, occupied a sixth part of the whole paper. So this was how they expanded his deed? Now he was the talk of the whole town, he who loved peace and solitude. And George would have a copy of the paper in his hand even before he crossed the frontier. Now he too would know about the murder. If only there were a learned censorship the paper would be half blank. Then people wouldn't find so much blue to read, further down. The second headline began with a V and close to it an R: Fire. Murder and arson lay waste the papers, the land, the minds—nothing attracts them more, if there's no fire after the murder their pleasure is incomplete; they'd like to start the fire themselves, they haven't the courage for murder, they're cowards; no one should read the papers; then they'd die of themselves, of a universal boycott.

Kien threw down the paper on the pile. He must cancel his regular order for papers at once. He left the hateful room. But it's night already, he said aloud, in the passage. How can I cancel my order? So as to go on reading, he took out his watch. All it offered was a dial. He could not make out the time. Murder and Arson were more forthcoming. In the library opposite there was light. He burned to know the time. He went into his study.

It was just eleven. No church bell was striking. Once it had been broad daylight. The yellow church was opposite. Across the little square people passed and repassed, excited. The hunchbacked dwarf was called Fischerle. He cried to soften a heart of stone. Paving stones jumped up and lay down again. There was a cordon of police round the Theresianum. Operations in charge of a major. He carried the warrant for arrest in his pocket. The dwarf had seen through it himself. Enemies had hidden under the stairs. Up above the hog was in charge. Books delivered over helpless to conscienceless beasts! The hog had composed a cookery book with a hundred and three recipes. It was said of his stomach—it had corners. Then why was Kien a criminal? Because he helped the poorest of the poor. For the police had drawn up a warrant even before they heard about the corpse. Against him all this gigantic levy. Forces on horse and on foot. Brand new revolvers, rifles, machine guns, barbed wire and tanks—but all is vain against him, they can't hang him till they've got him! Through their legs, they escape into the roses, he and his loyal dwarf. And now the enemy are on his heels, he hears grunting and panting, and the bloodhound at his throat. But ah, there is worse to come. On the sixth floor of the Theresianum the beasts are bidding each other good night; there they keep thousands of books unjustly in durance, tens of thousands, against their free will, guiltless, what can they do against the hog, cut off from *terra firma*, close under the Broiling attic roof, starving, condemned, condemned to the devouring Flames.

Kien heard cries for help. Despairing, he pulled at the cord which was attached to the skylight and the windows flew open. He listened. The cries redoubled. He mistrusted them. He hurried into the neighboring room and here too pulled at the cord. In here the cries were fainter. The third room echoed shrilly. In the fourth they could hardly be heard. He went back through all the rooms. He walked and listened. The cries rose and fell in waves. He pressed his hands against his ears and took them quickly away again. Pressed them and took them away. It sounded just the same as above. Ah, his ears were confusing him. He pushed the ladder, despite its resistant rails, into the middle of the study and climbed to its highest level. The upper part of his body overtopped the roof; he held fast on to the panes. Then he heard the despairing cries; they were the books screaming. In the direction of the

Theresianum he was aware of a reddish glow. Hesitantly it spread across the black gaping heavens. The smell of oil was in his nose. The glow of fire, screams, the smell; the Theresianum is Burning.

Dazzled, he closed his eyes. He lowered his burning skull. Drops of water splashed on his neck. It was raining. He flung his head back and offered his face to the rain. How cool—the strange water! Even the clouds were merciful. Perhaps they would put out the fire. Then an icy blow struck him on the eyelid. He was cold. Someone tweaked at him. They stripped him stark naked. They went through his all pockets. They left him his shirt. In the little mirror he saw himself. He was very thin. Red fruits, thick and bloated, grew all around him. The care-taker was one of them. The corpse attempted to talk. He would not listen to her. She was always saying: I ask you. He stopped up his ears. She tapped on her blue skirt. He turned his back on her. In front of him was seated a uniform without a nose. "Your name?" "Dr. Peter Kien." "Profession?" "The greatest living sinologist." "Impossible!" "I swear it." "Perjury!" "No!" "Criminal!" "I am in my right mind. I confess. In full possession of my senses. I killed her. I am perfectly sane. My brother knows nothing of it. Spare him! He is a famous man. I lied to him." "Where is the money?" "Money?" "You stole it." "I'm not a thief!" "Thief and murderer!" "Murderer!" "Thief and murderer!" "Murderer!" "You are under arrest. You will stay here!" "But my brother's coming. Leave me free until then! He must know nothing. I implore you!" And the caretaker steps forward, he is still his friend, and procures him a few days of liberty. He brings him home and keeps

guard over him, he does not let him out of the little room.
That was where George found him, in misery but not a
criminal. Now he is on his train already, if only he had
stayed here! He would have helped him at his trial! A
murderer must give himself up? But he won't. He will stay
here. He must watch the burning Theresianum.

Slowly he lifted his lids. The rain had stopped. The
reddish glow had paled, the fire brigade must have arrived
at last. The sky no longer rang with cries. Kien climbed
down from the ladder. In every room the cries for help
were stilled. So as not to miss them if they began again,
he left the skylights wide open. In the middle of the room
the ladder was placed ready. If the disaster should grow to
a climax, it would help his flight. Whither? To the Theresianum. The hog lay, a charred corpse, under the beams.
There, unknown among the crowd, there was much he
could do. Leave the house! Take care! Tanks are patrol-
ling the streets. All the king's horses. They think they
have caught him. The Lord will smite them; and he, the
murderer, will escape. But first he will efface all traces.

He kneels before the writing desk. He passes his hand
over the carpet. That was where the corpse lay. Is the blood
still visible? It is not visible. He pushed his fingers far into
his nostrils, but they only smell a little of dust. No blood.
He must look more closely. The light is bad. It hangs too
high. The flex of the table lamp does not reach so far. On
the writing desk is a box of matches. He strikes six at
once, six months, and lies down on the carpet. From very
close he holds the light to the carpet, looking for blood-
stains. Those red stripes are part or the pattern. They were
always here. They must be got rid of. The police will take

them for blood. They must be burned out. He presses the matches into the carpet. They go out. He throws them away. He strikes six new ones. Softly he passes them over one of the red stripes, then delicately pokes them in. They leave a brown mark behind them. Soon they go out. He strikes new ones. He uses a whole box. The carpet remains cool. It is marked all over with brownish scars. Glowing patches are here and there. Now nothing can be proved against him. Why did he confess? Before thirteen witnesses. The corpse was there too, and the ginger cat which can see at night. The murderer with wife and child. A knock. The police at the door. A knock.

Kien will not open. He stops his cars. He hides behind a book. It is on the writing table. He wants to read it. The letters dance up and down. Not a word can he make out. Quiet please! Before his eyes it flickers, fiery red. This is the aftermath of his terrible shock, on account of the fire, who would not have been frightened; when the Theresianum burns numberless numbers of books go up in flames. He stands up. How can he possibly read now. The book lies too far off. Sit! He sits again. Trapped. No, his home, the writing desk, the library. All are loyal to him. Nothing has been burned. He can read when he wants to. But the book is not even open. He had forgotten to open it. Stupidity must be punished. He opens it. He strikes his hand on it. It strikes twelve. Now I've got you! Read! Stop! No. Get out! Oh! A letter detaches itself from the first line and hits him a blow on the ear. Letters are lead. It hurts. Strike him! Strike him! Another. And another. A footnote kicks him. More and more. He totters. Lines and whole pages come clattering on to him.

They shake and beat him, they worry him, they toss him about among themselves. Blood, Let me go! Damnable mob! Help! George! Help! Help! George!

But George has gone. Peter leaps up. With formidable strength he grasps the book and snaps it to. So, he has taken the letters prisoner, all of them, and will not let them go again. Never! He is free. He stands up. He stands alone. George has gone. He has outwitted him. What does he know of the murder? A mental specialist. An ass. A wide-open soul. Yet he would gladly steal the books. He would want him dead soon. Then he'd have the library. He won't get it. Patience! "What do you want upstairs?" "Just to look round!" "Just to get round me!" That's what you'd like. Shoemaker stick to your idiots. He's coming again. In six months. Better luck next time. A will? Not necessary. The only heir will get everything he wants. A special train to Paris. The Kien library. Who collected it? The psychiatrist Georges Kien, who else? And his brother, the sinologist? Quite a mistake, there wasn't a brother, two of the same name, no connection, a murderer, he murdered his wife, Murder and Fire in all the papers, sentenced to imprisonment for life—for life—for death—the dance of death—the golden calf— an inheritance of a million—none but the brave—wave— parting—no—till death us do part—death by Fire—loss loss by Fire—burned burned by Fire—Fire Fire Fire.

Kien seizes the book on the table and threatens his brother with it. He is trying to rob him; everyone is out for a will, everyone counts on the death of his nearest. A brother is good enough to die, thieves kitchen of a world, men devour and steal books. All want something, and

all are gone, and no one can wait. Earlier they burned
a man's possessions with him, a will was nowhere to be
found and there was nothing left, nothing but bones. The
letters rattle inside the book. They are prisoners, they can't
come out. They've beaten him bloody. He threatens them
with death by fire. That is how he will avenge himself
on all his enemies! He has murdered his wife, the hog is
a charred skeleton, George will get no books. And the
police won't get him. Powerless, the letters are knocking
to be let out. Outside the police knock against the door.
"Open the door!" "Never more." "In the name of the law!"
"Pshaw!" "Let us in!" "Din." "At once." "Dunce." "You'll
be shot." "Pot." "We'll smoke you out!" "Lout!" They are
trying to break down his door. They won't do that easily.
His door is strong and fiery. Bang. Bang. Bang. The blows
grow heavier. He can hear them where he is. His door is
bolted with iron. But if the rust has eaten into the bolts?
No metal is all-powerful. Bang. Bang. Hogs are herded
before his door, ramming it with stomachs, with corners.
The wood will crack for certain. It looks so old and worn.
They seized the enemy trenches. Entrenched. Ready,
steady, crash. Ready, steady, crash! The bell. At eleven all
the bells ring. The Theresianum. The hunchback. March
off, pulling long noses. Am I right or am I not? Ready,
steady—am I right—ready, steady.

The books cascade off the shelves on to the floor. He
takes them up in his long arms. Very quietly, so that they
can't hear him outside, he carries pile after pile into the
hall. He builds them up high against the iron door. And
while the frantic din tears his brain to fragments, he
builds a mighty bulwark out of books. The hall is filled

with volume upon volume. He fetches the ladder to help him. Soon he has reached the ceiling. He goes back to his room. The shelves gape at him. In front of the writing desk the carpet is ablaze. He goes into the bedroom next to the kitchen and drags out all the old newspapers. He pulls the pages apart, and crumples them, he rolls them into balls, and throws them into all the corners. He places the ladder in the middle of the room where it stood before. He climbs up to the sixth step, looks down on the fire and waits.

When the flames reached him at last, he laughed out loud, louder than he had ever laughed in all his life.

Translated by C.V. Wedgwood

Negatives of My Father

Peter Henisch

IT'S NICE that you've come to see me, said my mother. You know, I've been so worried about Papa. He has to stay in the hospital at least two months this time, the doctors say, if all goes well. And if something doesn't go well, my God, I can't bear to think about it! When I remember how my father died—suddenly he was gone, and Grandma was alone in the empty apartment, with nothing but memories—it makes me cry.

You know, you simply get used to a person when you've been together so long. Sometimes in the evening after

---

PETER HENISCH (born in Vienna in 1943) studied German literature, philosophy, history, and psychology at the University of Vienna. For a time he belonged to a jazz band, and this musical background made him an enthusiastic admirer of the American rock star Jim Morrison, whose life he fictionalized in the novel *Morrisons Versteck* (Morrison's Hiding Place). Henisch became a freelance writer in 1971 and since then has produced numerous novels, plays, and poems, all of which deal with topical issues of the time such as the confrontation with Austria's Nazi past in *Die kleine Figur meines Vaters* (*Negatives of My Father*), present day Austrian anti-Semitism in *Steins Paranoia* (*Stein's Paranoia*) and the problems confronting immigrants in Vienna in *Der schwarze Peter* (Black Peter).

supper I feel like sitting at the kitchen table and reading the paper, because I haven't gotten to it all day because of the housework; Papa is already in bed and yells *Rosa, come on,* just because he's used to having me lying next to him. When I'm not lying next to him he feels irritated and can't get to sleep. That really gets on my nerves sometimes. But now, when I could sit for hours at the kitchen table and read the whole stack of newspapers which have piled up on the table during the last few weeks, I miss his calling Rosa. And then I suddenly hear the clock ticking or the faucet dripping, and I feel terribly lost. And then I go into the bathroom and do the hand laundry which is waiting for me there. Your brother isn't home any more, and at most I see your sister very early in the morning, but there never seems to be any less laundry. Or I'll stand at the sink and do the dishes which pile up there. There's not a soul here to eat and drink with me, but the mountain of dishes just keeps getting bigger. You know, when Papa walks in with muddy shoes right past the slippers I've laid out for him, or when he's eating cherries and spits the stones on the floor, instead of onto the plate I've set out for them, I can get really annoyed with him. I sometimes think, why do I torture myself? I clean and wash from morning till night, and he barely notices. But now, when I could do a really thorough housecleaning without any interruptions, and he wouldn't be there to interfere—now I don't get any joy out of it. And then I sit down at the table again and stare straight ahead for hours, and don't feel like doing anything at all.

What is it you'd like to do? Poke around in Papa's war papers? Well, I don't know what he'd say to that. But for all I care, go into the lab and look for what you need. He doesn't have to know. I think there are some letters from when he was in the army. You mustn't laugh at them, we were very young back then. Once Papa read parts of them to me. I had to laugh a little myself, a person changes so much.

So I went into the photo lab and took down from the bookshelf a file labeled December 1939–May 1940. After I had dusted it off with my sleeve, I opened it and began to leaf through the papers it contained. Letters, documents, memorabilia—the papers were yellowed, and first of all I had to get used to my father's handwriting, which was sometimes almost forbidding in its verticality. But after a while I could read it quite fluently, and became engrossed in the following letter: Dear Rosie, I still don't know where I'll be able to mail this, we are pushing on day and night, and I have no idea exactly where we're going. Anyway, I wouldn't be permitted to tell you even if I did know—you can understand that. I just want you to know that wherever I am, my thoughts are first and foremost with you. Please show this letter to my mother because it's uncertain when I'll get another chance to write. This train ride is extremely boring, our train is coupled with an endless convoy of trucks. We've been traveling now for almost two days, and your Walter would certainly not appeal to you at all, dirty and unshaven like this. At the railroad stations we get soup and tea from the Red Cross, NSV, and so forth. It's not much nor is it especially good, but the main thing is that it is warming. During the night it gets very cold in the unheated railroad cars, you see, and sleeping on the hard benches isn't the most comfortable either. Toward morning I sometimes get up and look out the window, but it's usually foggy and gray out there. But wherever we are—I'm a soldier now, Rosie, and I'm doing my duty. Even though leaving you was the hardest thing in the world, even if I almost cried yesterday afternoon— the *Führer* must know what he's doing.

I became involved with the Nazis, says my father's voice, through Mr. Albert Prinz, whose political views had been taking on increasingly sharp outlines as the years went by. In addition to his title as a supervising official he had recently acquired the title of Chief Battalion Commander. It was a lot like my photography: at first I didn't care one way or the other about my stepfather's political activity, any more than I had about his snapping pictures. And yet I ended up following in his political footsteps. And there is another parallel to my photographic career—it didn't really happen until after his death.

One day, at the age of about twelve, I told my father I wanted to join the Boy Scouts. My friend Franzl Ferlitsch had joined the Boy Scouts, you see, and since I didn't have any other friends, I said, I'll join too. The Boy Scouts— my father's voice snarls gruffly on the tape—why the Boy Scouts, of all things? On account of their hats—answers a timid childish voice—I want to join the Boy Scouts on account of their big hats! Besides, the Boy Scouts go for hikes in the woods, sing songs, and sit around campfires. Rubbish! says the surly voice. The Boy Scouts are connected to the Freemasons! You're going to join the German Gymnasts' Association, they hike and sing better, and they wear hats too.

The next morning Mr. Albert Prinz signed me up with

the German Gymnasts' Association. And even though I didn't realize it right away, since I had really only wanted to stay with my friend, the German Gymnasts' Association served the same purpose for me that the Boy Scouts would have. The uniform—the uniform played a tremendous role for me, you know. My dream was to be able to put on a uniform like a cloak of invisibility, and thereby to cease my existence as the Shrimp, which was all I had been up to that point.

The German Gymnasts wore really exotic hats, South-African style, and under that big hat I looked like a toadstool. But what I had found at last was a form of recognition as an equal among equals. In school I never found such recognition. In school I was always the smallest, the one the others looked down on.

Both at St. John's and at home I had acquired the habit of flinching whenever anyone made any kind of rapid movement. I had been beaten into submission, you know, and you have to remember that this expression sums up a whole process. My fellow pupils sensed my uncertainty, and my very uncertainty made them insecure in turn. And anyone who makes other people feel insecure and is *weak* in addition—is predestined for the role of the underdog.

One time after school a few of the other pupils tied me to the trunk of a solitary birch tree in Klagbaum Park, and ran off. Not until much later did some passersby, hearing my despairing cries, free me from this painful situation. Another time they literally put me up against the wall and nailed me there with snowballs. They didn't actually hit me; the exploding snowballs just outlined my silhouette, but it was still enough to make me want to scream.

In my helplessness I spat at one of my tormentors, and noticed what an effect that had. After that, whenever I felt even slightly threatened, I would roll my tongue into a little tube, take a deep breath, and make sure to hit my opponent on a sensitive place. With this suddenly discovered method of self-defense, however, I earned a name that really pained me, and it stuck with me through my entire time at the public school. *Poison Dwarf* the others would mock me, dodging my salvoes of saliva, and since no better response occurred to me than to spit again, I never could shake off that name.

The nickname Poison Dwarf was incidentally very similar to the nickname *Jewish Dwarf.* That's what the other kids called Grünzweig. He was a fellow pupil, also not especially tall, of the Mosaic persuasion. They also liked to taunt him with mocking verses, such as *Jew, Jew, spit in shoe.* But he had a way of ignoring them, either out of superiority or apathy.

On the basis of our external similarities—and above all because of the similarities in our positions, which were no positions at all—it would have seemed logical for us to join forces. That we didn't I attribute now to prejudice on both sides. He had had bad experiences with the Goyim, and he saw one in me. And for me the word Jew was a curse word, although I didn't actually have any idea why.

In any case, I had no friends among my classmates. And I don't know why Franzl Ferlitsch—he was the neighbor boy—wasn't ashamed, like all the others, to be my friend. Maybe it was because he had got to know me by myself during quiet games in the yard, from exchanging film-star cards away from the environment which made me insecure and which I in turn made insecure. In any case, because Franzl Ferlitsch didn't behave the way the others did toward me, I absolutely worshiped him.

Though we were the same age, he was two heads taller than I; and when I was permitted to walk at his side along the Heumühlgasse, I was exceedingly proud. See my friend, I exclaimed mentally to the schoolmates we passed, he's already more than five feet four inches tall! And he can box and toss knives, and with his right hand he can heft a cobblestone! And if you keep giving us such dumb looks, or chant any of those mean songs you've made up about me, he'll beat you up.

But that was outside of school. *In* school, it was sheer hell for me. If my relationship to my fellow students was difficult, my relationship to my teachers was no less so. To a certain degree their opinion of the pupil Hemis was even influenced by the opinion of my classmates. Or maybe it was the other way around—which came first, the chicken or the egg, I can't say.

For example, because of my small size people had the cruel preconception that I was a so-called sissy. The gym teacher, a certain Mr. Schmidt, was only too happy to perpetuate this prejudice. "You can't play soccer, Hemis, you're too weak for that! You can't even control the ball, you'll only get in the others' way!"

That the others called me a sissy precisely *because* I wasn't allowed to join in the soccer games, is obvious. But their attitudes—and particularly the attitude of the teachers—had an effect on me. So I suddenly became afraid of the horse or the rings *because* I was a sissy. More and more my character adapted to fit the caricature people had made of me.

But now, in the German Gymnasts' Association, I bravely choked back my fear of the horse and the rings. After the first time, when Mr. Albert Prinz had dragged me into the gym in the Schleifmühlgasse, with an iron grip and pithy admonitions about Germanic self-discipline, I actually came to enjoy going to my weekly gym classes. Above the entrance to the gym were the four big F's of the motto *Frisch, Fromm, Fröhlich und Frei* shaped into a swastika. The gymnasts were divided into squads of eight *men* each, and I was particularly proud to be so designated.

What I liked even more than the weekly gym lesson, though, were Sunday's Gymmasts' Association excursions in the Vienna Woods. We marched vigorously over hill and dale, sang patriotic songs, visited places sacred to the Father of Gymnasts, Ernst Jahn, and played at military scouting. "Armed with all our Power"/"We Fight for You, Oh German Woods"/ "No Nobler Death than 'midst the Foe," etc. With my *chin strap* pulled tight, contrary to regulations, I felt like Herman the German.

Herman the German was my favorite hero, I was really infatuated with him. Our teacher Kloss, the sole one of my teachers who was not antagonistic toward me, talked to us for hours on end about Herman the German. Kloss himself was small and puny, and probably for that reason there was a certain sympathy between us. Sometimes, when my stepfather had been putting particularly unbearable pressure on me again, I used to think, my father ought to be like Herr Kloss.

For his sake I memorized *The Grave in Busento* so perfectly that I still know it by heart today. (The voice of my
father on the tape quotes the first four lines of the ballad.)
I imagined the whole scene very vividly: The Goths with
their winged helmets, the night, the river . . . and how
they sink Alarich's coffin into the black waters, and how
they weep.

And for Kloss's sake I even wrote extra essays about *The
Battle in the Teutoburg Forest*, 9 A.D., that's still the only
historical date I'm really sure about. I would have liked
to be as strong, as big, as courageous as the Germanic
heroes. And if there had been any oppressors—Romans,
teachers, classmates or anyone else—I would have shown
them a thing or two!

Perhaps you can imagine a little—my father's voice says,
speaking about the war in France—what it meant to me
to be bigger and stronger than someone else for a change,
even if it was only in group formation. The others fled
before us for miles, and they brought the prisoners back
miles behind the front lines. And France, the country we
had expected something of, France, the archenemy, lay
down before us, as good as beaten. Beaten by me, too,
do you understand?—by my small contribution too—
that was quite a feeling! There follows a rather detailed
description of the deployment of the dive bombers, which
demoralized the French and tremendously strengthened
the morale of the German troops. With German thor-
oughness, my father says, we took over the American tac-
tic of safety first. Before every infantry or tank attack they
first bombed the objective into oblivion. That way, as soon
as we were ready to storm it, there wasn't any scrap of the

enemy left, so far as any human could foresee. And the French campaign was just one long triumphant advance, a single rush forward!

How proud Profesor Kloss would have been of us! We were following in the footsteps of Herman the German. And with what incredibly solid boots! German might would make the world right . . . On the other hand, there were some unpleasant sobering factors, especially in the pauses between the battles. Then memories of what had just happened would run through my brain, sometimes in slow-motion, sometimes speeded up—like a film. Human beings incinerating inside a tank, a farmhouse exploding into the air, a city being bombed . . . A child wearing a large military helmet which someone had plopped on his head, sitting among the ruins and playing with a doll . . . and they admonish you to conquer your inner cowardice, for Germany, for the future, for God knows what. And you have the feeling that if you conquer your inner cowardice, your outer cowardice will emerge. People found various means of suppressing this feeling. For one it was enthusiasm, for another alcohol. For me it was photography.

From the German Gymnasts' Association, says my father's voice, I transferred *more or less automatically* into the Hitler Youth. Most of my friends joined after a certain time, and naturally I wanted to go with them. That won't work, my stepfather objected. For a moment that pulled me up short. But in those early years one could fulfill the requirement of being an Aryan by simply making a declaration under oath.

I entered an apprenticeship. A brief guest appearance

in secondary school had ended in a flop. That's what I
expected all along, said Mr. Albert Prinz, and he condemned me to learn to be a barber. Like father, like son—
so the son, too, was to learn to cut hair. At least he should
be able to run a comb through someone's hair . . . But to
find a decent barber's apprenticeship in the depression
years around 1930 was no easy matter. And particularly
not if a person looked like a little boy, as I did. My father
dragged me from one barbershop to another. Finally a
Master Bernegger on Zollergasse declared his willing-
ness to give *the little fellow* a chance.

He was clearly not overjoyed with me. The *little fellow* was much too dreamy for the Master Barber. When
I speak to Walter, he doesn't hear me. Or he hears me
and is so startled he drops something . . . Old Bernegger was himself a senile old granddad, and behind the
times—you could see that from the decor of his shop. He
probably kept me on only because he couldn't get a better
apprentice. I brushed the hair from the customers' collars
and dried their faces. During the day I washed out the
shaving basin, and at the end of the day I swept out the
shop.

I never actually reached the point of cutting a customer's hair all on my own, even right up to when I took
the journeyman's examination. The only thing the Master
finally permitted me to do was to shave people. It was
shaving, however, that I was most terrified of. It cost me
an effort just to take hold of the razor, a sharp, potentially
lethal instrument. And I was terrified of the beards old
Bernegger gave me to shave. He didn't trust me with the
finer beards. He had no compunctions, however, about

abandoning the coarser beards to treatment, or mistreat-
ment, at my unskilled hands. Even now I recall my only
regular customer with particular revulsion. Kratochwyl
was his name, and he usually came staggering directly
from the bar across the street . . .

You can imagine, after such a promising beginning,
that I wasn't wild to spend the rest of my life as a barber.
Once I had the journeyman's examination behind me, I
volunteered for the army. They didn't take me—according to one of my father's accounts, because of *inadequate
height* or, according to another, because I had *two registered
addresses.* So I signed up for the Labor Service. I wanted
to get away from all I had been through—the homes, St.
John's, the schools, my parents, the apprenticeship—but
I had no idea where to go. So at first I worked on the
Wallsee Dam on the Danube, and on the regulation of
the Lech, which in those days was still a wild mountain
brook.

The Labor Service was just like the Army—primarily
a haven for the unemployed. In our uniforms—gray right
down to the underwear—we looked like shabby gasmen.
But I wore even this uniform with a certain joy and a
certain pride. Just for the sake of belonging to some kind
of group, I probably would have been willing to slip into
a uniform with blue polka dots.

I think back to my father's letters from the front, in
which he writes of his *beautiful black tank uniform.* And
I think of all the photos which show him in uniform:
wasn't I a good-looking fellow?—Not long ago, says his
voice on the tape, I photographed a national rally of the
Red Falcons. You'll laugh, but when they dressed me up

for a joke in an Ancient Falcon's uniform, it gave me a bit of a thrill.

In the Labor Service I was still only a simple *workman*. Above me were foremen, camp commanders, chief camp commanders, field commanders, and the devil only knows what else. But I was on the same level as the others. Through work, I had become their equal.

Only one of them didn't want to accept me. His name was Schejbal, or Schebésta. He looked like a butcher. Big and very pink. With hands like soup bowls.

Are you a yid? he asked provocatively. Shorty, kinky-haired! Only eat kosher meat? Stink of onions? Write with your left hand? Go to temple on the Schabbes? Lost your foreskin?

The guy made me furious. I would have loved to open my fly. And show him my member. Look, you moron! Look at my peter. Who says I'm circumcised!

But actually I wanted to tell you about the Hitler Youth. My membership there was inactive during my time in the Labor Service. And when I returned from the Labor Service Mr. Albert Prinz had died and there was no money in the house. I had other worries then. But later, when I was already working as a photographer, people suddenly considered it important to remind me of my membership in the Hitler Youth. And as a result my contact with the Hitler Youth intensified.

One day I was sitting in the photo laboratory of the firm of Ernst & Hielscher, putting together demo photos, when a couple of faces came down the steps. They looked somehow familiar, but I wasn't sure from where. And one of them came up to me, bared his teeth in a smile, and clapped me on the shoulder in a comradely fashion. The Prinz Boy, he said, grinning incessantly, the successor of our unforgettable friend and comrade-in-arms, very good, very good! And then the funeral of my stepfather came into my mind, and I recalled the faces, even without the mourning bands . . .

—The funeral of your stepfather . . . the death of your stepfather . . . What was that like?—I hear my own voice on the tape. When did Mr. Albert Prinz actually die, and of what?—Oh, you mean I haven't told you about that? asks my father's voice, very audibly surprised. I could have sworn I had already told you that.

All right, listen. It was the morning I had returned home from the Labor Service. I remember it as though it were yesterday. It was snowing in thick flakes, and the wind blew the snow almost horizontally. And I came around the corner from the Naschmarkt, and past the gas streetlight which still stood opposite the entrance to our house. And I remember—this detail is important—that I was whistling and singing.

And I stepped into the house entrance, and the manager objected to my whistling and singing, referring to a sad event which he at first didn't specify more clearly than that. But what's happened? I asked. And then he reported to me haltingly the sudden and presumably tragic death of Mr. Albert Prinz. When I suddenly grasped the sense of his words, I left him standing there and ran up the stairs, two or three steps at a time, in order to get to my mother on the third floor as soon as possible. My stepfather had died on New Year's Eve, of all times, and, of all things, of a heart attack, in a so-called compromising situation . . .

No, says my father's voice in a suddenly altered tone. What I just told you can't be right. When I got back from the Lab or Service it was autumn, not winter. The wind was driving dried leaves through the streets, not snow. When I got back from the Labor Service, my stepfather was still alive.

So the day when I heard of the sudden and presumably tragic death of Mr. Albert Prinz must have been later. But I know for certain that I heard of it in the morning, and on a New Year's morning on top of that. At that time I wasn't living with my parents, but rather in a room I was subletting, not far from their apartment. And on New Year's morning I came whistling and singing into the hallway of the house at 12 Heumühlgasse to wish them a Happy New Year.

But suddenly the door to the manager's apartment opened, and the manager says to me—I can still hear these words in my ear, Hey, Walter, don't sing! And why *shouldn't* I sing? I asked, and the manager said, your *father*, he said, died today. And for an instant it was totally empty and white inside my head. I simply couldn't get those words into my head. And then I ran up the stairs to my mother, taking two or three steps at every bound.

In late afternoon the police asked me to come to the morgue. There he lay, this *colossus* whom I had feared throughout my childhood and youth. They told me that he had died in a hotel in the Josefstadt district, a downright impertinently lovely death. The bullet which had been circulating in his body since the days of Verdun struck his heart at precisely the best moment.

Naturally the body of Mr. Albert Prinz was cremated,

as befits a proper German corpse. A lot of his party comrades appeared at the funeral, or rather cremation service,
of the man who had died so unexpectedly. These party
comrades had no inkling of the existence of a wife, let
alone a son of their dear departed companion. What,
you're *the Prinz boy?* they asked me, with evident amaze-
ment, well, what's your name?—I calculate that my father,
at the time when his stepfather died, must already have
been over twenty years old.

What do you want to know, my grandmother asked,
how tall my departed husband was? Well let's see, how
tall was he? I guess he was about as tall as you are. Yes,
five-seven and a half, if you're five-seven and a half then
he probably was too. What do you mean, that's not tall
at all? Now listen here, in our family he was practically a
giant!

But stop asking such irrelevant questions and let's talk
about something important, now that you're here. For a
long time I've wanted to talk to you about certain things,
but you never have the time! I'm an old woman. I could
die any day. It's good if I get my affairs in order ahead of
time. Here in the drawer are all of my documents, plus my
insurance policy and a savings book with a little money
for the burial.

Good heavens, if I relied on the rest of you for this
sort of thing, I'd probably have to walk out to the Central Cemetery! And bless my soul, if it were up to me, I
wouldn't mind at all. But unfortunately things aren't as
well organized with us humans as they are among the
elephants. So you'll have to have me driven out there,
low-budget, of course, but what must be, must be.

But here's the most important thing: here, in this envelope, pay attention when I'm talking to you, I have something else for you, something special. A nice big Proof of Aryan Descent. We got it for you way back, right after you were born. What do you mean, you don't want any Aryan document? You never can tell whether you might not need it again. Nobody asked us back then whether we *wanted* an Aryan document, but when we finally had one, we thanked God, believe me!

Good God, what a lot of excitement there was when Hitler came. You have to give him credit though, he did a lot of good things. It can't be denied, he did put our house in order, and if a person wasn't afraid to work, he could get work. But suddenly we all needed that old document. Praise be to God, my sister in Hollabrunn, your great-aunt, had a way with words and a little spare cash. She ran all over creation, to the most distant parishes, she corresponded with any foreign country we still had contact with. Don't ask what people wanted of her. Don't ask what she had to put up with; if she hadn't been there, well, it would have been all up with you, curtains, so there . . .

Where was I, asks my father's voice on the tape. Oh yes, I was talking about the funeral guests in the Ernst & Hielscher photo lab, baring their teeth and clapping me on the shoulder and invoking the unforgettable people's comrade Albert Prinz in Valhalla.—And now you're a rising star in the photographic sky, isn't that right, and you're still on the old membership lists of the Hitler Youth, right? You might work for our common goal, right? *One Folk, One Reich, One Führer.* You certainly don't want to let yourself be exploited by these miserable Jews, right? Yes, you'll think where you really belong before it's too late, right? Or your poor father will be turning over in his grave!

We'll give you any amount of photographic supplies you need, right, not to mention new equipment, right? And a new starting point for a better future. Because tomorrow, you know, everything here will be heaved overboard, because tomorrow, you know—your elegant employers will be disposed of, *For today Germany's Ours*, but tomorrow . . .

This offer, says my father, was too enticing. It would have been impossible to turn down this offer. The Nazis, his voice says, not without pride, had, as you can see, a good nose for young talent. They were looking for good propagandists like the proverbial needle in the haystack. And besides, accepting this offer seemed to me belatedly fulfilling a bequest from Mr. Albert Prinz. I hated my stepfather so much while he was alive that I could have killed him, but now that he was dead I felt a filial piety which increased with every day that passed.

From that time on I photographed for the Hitler Youth. And there were unprecedented photos to take. Marching youths and girls, fluttering flags . . . eyes full of faith, singing mouths, raised arms . . . Those were simply *pictures* for me, do you understand? And the movement just swept me along with it. To sing "Those hollow bones are quaking" was lovely. "One for all, all for one, strength through joy."

Not only did I *belong*. Now, among a lot of similar people, I was in an exposed position. So to speak a favorite son of the party. *The photographer from headquarters*, no longer just Shrimp.

You ask whether I had any pangs of conscience after I learned the whole truth about my ancestry. Sure, of course. But tell me: What should I have done? Should I have gone there and given myself up? I shoot photos for you, but I'm not *allowed* to?—I was already much too deeply involved in the whole mess. I couldn't have simply walked away from the whole thing. And if I had tried that, what would have happened? Heavens, son, it's easy for you to talk . . .

Besides, I was naive, you see; that business about the putsch attempt, for instance—I really didn't understand it right up to the last moment. After the putsch attempt we were illegal for a while, so I photographed out of a position of illegality. I simply photographed what people got for me. *For me the photographing was always the main thing, and everything else was secondary.* And perhaps the photographing also gave me a chance to *look away from events by viewing them through the camera*, for all I know.

And then one day I photographed Josef Goebbels in the Sofia chambers. And at a press conference following his lecture, he shook my hand. And it occurred to me that he was barely taller than I was. Yes, yes, we little chaps, he said, as if he had guessed my thoughts, we can be great, too, if we're put in the right place. After that I felt I was in the right place.

As for the rest, during this period my father went down the Danube with his friend Trude, in his collapsible kayak Sonny, from Melk, Krems, or Klosterneuburg. They camped on lonely islands in the Danube, and from his tent waved a pennant whose emblem—a white bolt of lightning on a black field—had nothing at all to do with the runes used by the SS. Trude, he says, was a good companion, an excellent swimmer, and a passionate woman. The fact that she was tiny struck me, as you can imagine, not as a handicap, but as a virtue. We were together for over two years, and if I hadn't met your mother, we would probably have married.

My father met my mother in the Opitz Drugstore on Gudrunstrasse, where he worked for a short while in the photo lab. She mistook him for a clerk and asked him for a chamois leather brush. To this day, for my father, a chamois leather brush is the symbol of their love. I'm a *photographer*, my father said, I'll take the most beautiful pictures of you. You have lovely eyes, my father said, I can see myself mirrored in them.

And then, says my father, the Germans marched into Austria. Seen as an *action*, as a *show*, their entry was a thoroughly imposing thing. In this respect when compared to the Socialists and even more to the conservatives, the Nazis were remarkable. They did something for your senses, especially for your eyes, and therefore for the camera.

Just take the famous "Home to the Reich" proclamation on the Heldenplatz. I was posted right at the outer castle gate. Each of us had his precise orders. *The pictures were much more important than the reality.*

Get us pictures of laughing, cheering people. Even if you have to force them to laugh and cheer!—But that wasn't necessary at all. The reality was more than sufficient for the pictures.

For never before have *extras* performed so voluntarily. Even sitting up on the statues of the horses of Prinz Eugen and the Archduke Karl, they cheered themselves hoarse. We want to see our *Führer!* The *Führer* let them roar, up to a certain climax. And then he stepped out onto the famous balcony and his appearance took that climax and intensified it further. And then thousands of arms went up, and thousands of swastika flags. And the ecstasy was much more ecstatic than at any pop concert. The people virtually had tears streaming down their faces . . . Never have I had such ideal models.

Translated by Anne Close Ulmer

The Strudlhof Steps
Heimito von Doderer

IN THE MEANTIME René had reached the corner of the Strudlhofgasse and had stopped there. Slanting sunlight could still be seen like a thick, porous carpet over every visible plane. Here at the corner, the sunlight reached into the gap and the treetops behind it. The buildings of the University Institutes of Physics and Radiology on the right-hand side stood smooth and shuttered with their incomprehensible contents, breathing that new kind of romanticism which issues most strongly from the most

---

HEIMITO VON DODERER (1896–1966) returned to Vienna in 1920 when released as a prisoner of war in Siberia and earned his doctorate in history in 1925. His early works aroused little response, but after serving again in the military in World War II, he enjoyed his first critical success with the novel *Die Strudelhofstiege* (*The Strudlhof Steps*). A slow and painstaking writer of long, involved novels, Doderer devoted 25 years to his masterpiece *Die Dämonen* (*The Demons*). His writings provide a critical insider's portrayal of Viennese bourgeois and aristocratic society during the interwar period, describing how they lived in Vienna and how they vacationed, the bourgeois in various summer spas and the aristocrats in the Semmering area. Doderer demonstrates that the human being cannot adapt life to thought but can only successfully adapt thought to life.

exact sciences, as if in the emanation their essence were transformed into its opposite, as it were.

The direction in which René Stangeler was walking had no connection with his way home. This direction might only be called "away-from-home." The condition of bemused subjectivity René was in will be thought appropriate for a young man. But in his case age has much less to do with it than we might think at first glance. The same condition was a characteristic of the grown-up members of his family too; it was, in fact, the basis of their everyday life. Just as René on his walk to the Strudlhof Steps now didn't expect anything less than the extraordinary, so too did his brothers and sisters believe it to be their due at all times, so to speak, a standard they expected all their lives; they shied away from any other. And these people, who could compass many things, would never yet achieve one thing, that of existing as quite ordinary human beings.

René walked down slowly, enjoying it and forgetting to meditate. Along the slope the crowns of several trees were crowded together. The steps led downward in a leisurely way but descended surprisingly deep. There was a smell of earth here.

At the bottom we come into the Liechtensteinstrasse and Stangeler went along it to the left, where it soon connects up with a wider arterial road near a tavern called The Flight into Egypt. René knew this road, of course, and the moment of knowledge disturbed him, as if a lateral brightness had intruded upon his dream, which he now gathered around him like a coat as if a draught might sweep inside. He quickly crossed the Alserbachstrasse

and continued along the Liechtensteinstrasse which had
become much narrower now.

This road seemed to be the boundary between two very
different parts of the city, which gazed at each other like
two strangers across the narrow gap. One side looking
down on the other from above, that is: for initially the
land on which the houses were built rose high on the left
side, as in the whole of this area, and then there were
cheap new buildings four or five stories high on this side
of the road; while the right-hand side consisted mostly of
small one-story houses, of which only a few might be less
than a hundred years old. This part of the city is called
"Liechtenthal," and it was familiar home-ground to Franz
Schubert, who had once been the organist at Liechtenthal
parish church. But René Stangeler never knew things like
this and wouldn't have enjoyed hearing about them now
either. Although he was a thorough-minded man, he was
fundamentally uneducated—we might say that in the
foundations of his being he was the exact opposite of a
product like, for instance, Major, later Colonel, Laska,
who once took Lieutenant Melzer on a bear hunt.

Now the street came to an end. René was standing at
the top of the steps.

Stangeler knew his native city relatively little and this
part almost not at all. Nightly excursions on which he
ventured quite often—just like his sister Etelka, only
alone even at that time—led him again and again only
into the bars and cafés of the First District, of the Inner
City, that is, or into the haunts of artists near his parents'
house on the Praterstrasse. The slight surprise that René
now felt at the upper end of the Strudlhof Steps blended

into his romantic notions, dotted the i's on his whole
mood as it were, which for this small reason became dis-
proportionately intensified. It seemed to him that here
was revealed a real live stage on which he longed to play a
role to his taste, and while he was looking down over the
steps and the terraces, in a flash he immediately recorded
in the depths of his mind a scene that could be acted here;
of course it was a crucial one, an ascent, a descent and a
meeting halfway, wholly operatic.

In short, it was one of those scenes that we remember
only from the stage, but which in life actually happen,
though rarely, and then they occur completely unexpectedly. And it is only afterward that we recognize them as
such.

A little lane branched off the road to the right. On
one of the corner houses, René now noticed, not too high
up, just above the ground floor on the wall of the first
floor, there was a round bas-relief finished in blue glaze,
representing a unicorn.

He had paused halfway across the side-lane and was
looking up at the unicorn when he heard steps behind
him which now slowed down and stopped.

René turned around and saw a girl of about seventeen
in a simple gray suit, holding a portfolio under her arm.

At the same moment he laughed and the laughter was
an astute move and provided without any strain the link
he instantly sought: for she, also laughing, looked up at
the unicorn and said:

"D'you know what sort of queer animal that is,
exactly?"

"A unicorn," Stangeler answered. He could see now that

she had dark red hair, which curled attractively around her temples under her gray sailor hat. The temples themselves were very white, pale, and matte like her face, in which the eyes were somewhat slanted (similar to René's, though of course this didn't occur to him).

"But did something like that really exist once?" she asked.

"Yes—probably," Stangeler said and thought of Julius Caesar's descriptions of ancient Germania. "But my dear Fräulein," he added quickly, going on at a fast rate so that the words came out naturally and innocently, "if you will allow me to tell you more about it, it would give me great pleasure—only I should like to talk in the big pastry shop on the other side of the Alserbachstrasse. Because I'm in dire need of refreshment at the moment. May I invite you? They have marvelous chocolate doughnuts with whipped cream."

Having lately stepped over the threshold between boyhood and young manhood, he had already achieved something like a mechanical assurance in his dealings with female beings, with whom by the way he was almost fully conversant on the salient point. Any, even distant opportunities of that sort were never at any time ignored by René: and even at this time, in this early, even first selection there was evident in him the occasional inclination of all the Stangelers for all that was good-natured and innocent, and also intellectually inferior to their way of thinking; they needed both of these qualities as a sounding board for the sense of their own worth, and with this spice they were probably able to enjoy this or that experience so much more, just as in certain dishes nutmeg and curry powder seem necessary to some people.

Our couple in the meantime have crossed the main road and reached the pastry shop and were not without sustenance there, for René was in funds, despite his meager pocket money. A large, forgotten bookcase, standing in a corner of the landing on the second floor of his parents' house, was the source of this; it was stuffed in disorderly fashion with all the novels of the eighties, in particular with the works of a certain Georg Eber, distinguished in linen and gilt-edges. This bookcase was hollowed out slowly by René, starting from the back, just as trees in Africa are hollowed out by termites starting from within. His relations with several book dealers were on a regular footing.

Now, however, instead of starting in his usual way by unpacking his sample case of interesting and original things and arranging his store window, as it were, something completely different came over him here at this little marble table, occasioned by the relaxed mood and the ease of his afternoon: a calmness of being superior to the clockwork routine that was usually brought into play to impress a girl. It now seemed to René quite impossible to encircle this opportunity in a firm grip, and perhaps for the first time in his life he felt indifferent to the impression he might or might not make. This feeling—comparable to someone sitting down in an extremely deep and comfortable armchair which physically prevents him from getting up—was very distinct, and was quite new to him. He welcomed it with a deep joy and with the remarkable desire to go on living like this forever.

"And now, what about unicornies?" she asked and put down her cup of hot chocolate. "Oh yes, unicorns," said René; he gazed at the girl and said nothing more.

"I think you only want to eat—telling me about them is too boring for you at the moment," she said, smiling.

"I don't feel at all bored," he replied with a meaningful emphasis, as it were, and gazing quietly in front of him, he contemplated her head framed against the background of the street that was in movement to and fro outside behind the big plate glass window.

"Well, the unicorns, now, or unicornies as you so charmingly call them, it is quite probable that they did exist. Last century, everything that didn't fit into a scientific framework was held to be mere nonsense, just fables and legends—since then, though, many more strange new animals have been discovered, and nowadays people no longer think of the fabulous creatures as being purely fabulous. Every one of them was based on one or another kind of truth, basilisks, dragons, and unicorns." "Are you a student?"

"Yes. The unicorn was a wild and ferocious animal which lived alone in impenetrable forests. But it was very easy to catch." "Oh, why?" she asked, more surprised, really, than pert; the latter tone didn't seem very much in her line, it was only a mechanically presented rampart of her character borrowed, copied for quick self-defense.

"You had to have a virgin," said Stangeler, "but she had to be genuine." He felt a certain helplessness at the present switching of the points in the line of conversation which had resulted from the subject itself, and he now observed this turn on to risqué matters—which he usually reached quite quickly at other times—with an awareness that he wasn't able to help taking that line for the moment. It was like a momentary numbness. And out of it he noticed, as something he had expected all the time, her mouth—not a small mouth, but rather a wide mouth—curving to one side, expressing her hesitation between her true manner and the mimic and well-worn gestures that were second nature to other girls of her age. "And what did the virgin do with the unicorny?"

"She had only to sit down in the forest where the unicorn lived—and it quickly came up to her, sank on its knees before her and put its head quite tamely in her lap. And then you could tie it up and lead it away, and it would never once resist."

"Come, come, that's a story, if you like," she said now, trying to resist a feeling rising within her that here she had unexpectedly happened to touch upon something quite new and fascinating: because of the small coincidence of having been in a good mood on her way home from her employer's office (a lawyer's, where she had been a typist for the last two years), because a difficult case had been successfully concluded, a lot of work had been finished, and the lawyer—in a good mood himself, of course,— had praised her unstintingly and had promised her a not insignificant increase in pay: and because of the good mood, she had spoken to this boy in front of the house called the "Blue Unicorn" quite spontaneously, having always been curious about what sort of animal the blue sheep up there really was. But now, and not least because Stangeler had not pursued the branch opened up by the switch in the lines of conversation, she felt the borders of a new terrain bubbling up and pulling at her with a gentle yearning, a terrain for her completely on the other side, and a wind blew through her whole being, rustling over all the leaves of all the novels she had ever read.

So these two children of very different banks and zones of life sat over cups of chocolate and chocolate doughnuts with whipped cream—Stangeler, by the way, drank coffee and was smoking a cigarette, a thing they don't usually like in pastry shops anywhere, but the waitress had permitted it, since it was only a short while to the evening closing time. Outside, the street had long ago been submerged in a fine, even gray, in which the first lights were swimming; everything was tired though still busy, aching from the day. And it was some time since Paula Schachl, without any direct transition, had begun to talk about herself: about her employer and the big lawsuit that had just finished (a car factory versus its timber supplier, and therefore rather out of Stangeler's range), about the praise she had received today after all the work she'd put in, sometimes until nine or ten o'clock at night, about her aunt with whom she was living (here in Liechtenthal, by the way), and finally about a physician, a Dr. Brandeis, who was treating her at the outpatient department of the General Hospital; yesterday she had gone there once again, he was a very nice man and extremely conscientious. In the winter she had sprained her left ankle by turning her foot on some slippery ice and had done something to the ligaments.

They left the pastry shop and walked toward this old quarter; Paula had hardly paused in her story all this time. Now she was talking about her various girlfriends

and acquaintances, all of whom seemed to live in this
area; and on Sunday mornings apparently there seemed to
be a customary stroll along the Nussdorferstrasse where
they would all meet. René, too, was now standing on the
threshold of a different world, so to speak, which appeared
to him to be not without delights, and he glanced into it,
even with a certain longing, but only rather incidentally
and as if out of the corner of his eye. He perceived dimly
that they lived easier, better, and much more sensible
lives in that world. But this was the only part of Paula's
conversation which he grasped as something graphic and
actual. For the rest he listened to her as if she were singing wordlessly: a long song based on a short melody with
occasional ritornellos, a song that remained the same
and hung suspended in the air, like certain insects that
hover in the same spot with a humming note. Just so
was that even song with its ritornellos suspended before
the background of the wide street, and then it hovered
where the cheap tall houses and the little old houses stood
faring each other, and then at the street corner with the
blue unicorn. All this, while being gradually engulfed
between strings of lights in the now dark evening, took
on a solidity, now dense, now fluid, set in depth against
an illuminated framework like a golden backcloth: the
steps! the Strudlhof Steps! the real, live stage of dramatic
appearances, with drums beating and trumpets sounding,
and it was just to this, to this alone, that Paula's light
singing had an affinity in Stangeler's mind.

Her soft-voiced rather plaintive solo, with that particular monotony that characterizes, say the *cor anglais*, was
performed in its lonely way, as if against the forceful *tutti*

of an orchestra, before the background of the torn cleft that shone like gold: of all this she could have no notion, Stangeler thought, and it was just that which seemed to him important and touching. But René was wrong. Just as the insubstantial and the vaguely romantic had power over him, it also had power over her, in whom the leaves of a chaos of books were rustling. We don't need to discuss the standards of either side: whether Puccini or a two-penny novel, here it meant the same. It seems to us, though, that during all these events, more was evolving in René than in her.

But now they had to part. They had already agreed upon their next meeting. Her aunt lived around the corner.

—Translated by Gudrun Gomori and Barbara Marshall

Vienna Passion

Lilian Faschinger

ON THE DAY I saw Magnolia Brown for the first time, my mother woke me at three thirty-three in the morning. And for the first time I held it against her.

I'd been suffering from a very nasty attack of bronchial catarrh for the last four days, going out only to buy medicines from the St Mary Magdalene Pharmacy on the corner of Kettenbrückengasse and Rechte Wienzeile and to visit the produce stalls in the Naschmarkt for a piece

LILIAN FASCHINGER (born in Tschöran, Carinthia, in 1950) earned a doctorate in English Literature at the University of Graz in 1979. After teaching there, she became a freelance writer and translator in 1992, dividing her time between Vienna and Paris. For her novels, short prose narratives, poetry, plays, and translations from English into German, she has received numerous literary awards and prizes. She attracted critical prominence and popular attention with her picaresque novel *Magdelena Sünderin* (*Magdelena the Sinner*) with its racy story of a seductress who avoids lengthy relationships by murdering the men. In *Wiener Passion* (*Vienna Passion*) Faschinger addresses the major contemporary topic of multiculturalism in past and present Vienna by portraying the life of an attractive black slave. The narrator is her great granddaughter who has traveled to Vienna to investigate the life of her celebrated forebear.

of beef fillet, a large marrowbone, some potherbs and a couple of onions, the ingredients for good nourishing beef broth. Good nourishing beef broth is the only food I can take when I have one of these dangerous infections, which have been plaguing me as long as I can remember. All my life I've had inadequate immunity to viruses, and in winter I'm a martyr to assorted colds and chills practically the whole time. If I go to my regular coffee house, the Café Anzengruber in Schleifmühlgasse, and there's only a seat near the door free, it's almost a cast-iron certainty that the draught entering with every new customer will give me acute bronchitis within a couple of days, keeping me bedridden for days on end. If I have to stand in a crowded tram in cold, wet weather I can expect a nasty attack of catarrhal tonsillitis. If I come home late at night in early December, making my way, lost in thought, past the empty stalls of the Naschmarkt, the gusts of autumnal wind typical of Vienna, reinforced by the architectural bottleneck there, are bound to trigger a bout of flu with a high temperature and a muzzy feeling that may have been brewing for quite some time, and was just waiting for its chance to develop.

Of course Vienna, with its dreaded Viennese wind and alarmingly low temperatures in winter, isn't the place where someone of my delicate constitution ought to be living at all. The pharmacist in the St Mary Magdalene Pharmacy, a sensitive woman who genuinely understands vulnerable natures like mine, says I ought to go south like the swallows around the feast of the Birth of Our Lady in early September, and come back at Lady Day in late March. Did I never think, she asked that day, of going to Madeira like our Empress Elisabeth back in the past, the island climate there did wonders for Empress Sisi's infected lungs, in her opinion the secret lies in Madeira's volcanic origins, quite recently she read a scientific article in her trade paper, *The Lady Pharmacist's Companion,* supporting the theory that the felicitous combination of volcanic phenomena with a maritime climate will cure people who are chronically susceptible to colds. Or if Madeira is too far to go, she suggested, I could try the Lipari Islands, Stromboli is probably another very healthy place, likely to stabilize easily inflamed respiratory passages. There is obviously great healing power in the mysterious combination of volcanic and maritime features, she said, fire and water, two opposing elements existing side by side. I refrained from contradicting the pharmacist, who seems to be well informed and always listens patiently to accounts of my lamentable state of health, I merely pointed out that my meager income didn't allow me to take such long trips, Empress Sisi had had entirely different opportunities at her command, why, Queen Victoria herself placed a ship at Sisi's disposal for the voyage to Madeira, a measure upon which the Vienna Regional Health Insurance scheme is hardly likely to decide even if a person's membership premiums have been paid on the dot for decades. At this point the pharmacist's young assistant joined in the conversation, saying that when her uncle contracted a nasty case of pneumonia all of a sudden, just like that, the Vienna Regional Health Insurance paid up without a murmur for a Mediterranean cruise, second class, so cruises for the sake of your health aren't anything unusual, and her uncle landed in Trieste three weeks later with his lungs perfectly well again. Here the old lady from the building at 14 Kettenbrückengasse, who had just come into the pharmacy with her toy spaniel, raised her failing voice and said Empress Sisi was nothing but a malingerer, there was evidence to prove it, and who, pray, paid for the Empress's expensive trips when she imagined herself unwell but the ordinary people of the Austro-Hungarian monarchy, victims bled dry by those vampires of the imperial house, victims including her late father, a man who had held the reputable position of retired stipendiary councillor in the civil service at the time of his death, and where would we be if we went running to the health insurance scheme for every little ailment, her late father had suffered his painful rheumatism without a word of complaint, and for years she herself had tried to alleviate her far from imaginary rheumatoid arthritis with medicinal herbs laboriously gathered in the Vienna woods, she did think one might show a little solidarity toward people who really were severely ill.

I asked the three ladies to let me finish what I was saying, and explained that quite apart from the fact that it was financially impossible for me to take long trips abroad, my pupils kept me in the city, and anyway I loved Vienna.

But of course you love Vienna, cried the pharmacist, the old lady and the pharmacist's assistant, of course you do, it isn't only the Viennese who love Vienna, the whole world loves Vienna, you have only to look at the statistics for overnight stays published by the Viennese hotel trade to see that. They themselves, although they hadn't been born in Vienna, loved the place dearly, you didn't have to be a native of Vienna like me to love it with all your heart and feel the deepest affection for the city.

Yes, naturally you love Vienna. You love it as dearly as your own mother, even if the harsh climatic conditions in Vienna in autumn and winter don't make such a depth of affection easy for a person susceptible to bronchial asthma.

After I'd bought a small bag each of violet leaf tea, lime flower tea, and dead nettle tea in the St Mary Magdalene Pharmacy, as well as two little bottles of *atropinum sulfuricum* D3 and *arsenicum* D6, I went back to the Death House. I walked slowly, stopping as usual for a short rest in the tobacconist's on the corner of Kettenbrückengasse and Schöbrunnerstrasse, because in the long term chronic colds have a dreadfully debilitating effect on the organism. Usually I sit down on the folding chair near the little iron stove and have a chat with the lady in the tobacconist's about preventative health measures in general, since she isn't by any means blessed with a robust physical constitution either. That day, however, I saw with some annoyance that the lady in the tobacconist's was already sitting on the folding chair herself, and before I got any chance to describe my own symptoms she began complaining about the unbearable back pain which was making it quite impossible for her to stand behind the counter. I leaned against a pile of copies of the weekly magazine *Profile*, because I was fighting off a nasty stitch in my side as a result of the effort of walking, and advised the lady in the tobacconist's to seek medical advice at once, to which she replied that she couldn't leave the tobacconist's just like that, her tobacconist's shop was a place where people liked to meet, and moreover the locals had a right to their daily newspapers and their tobacco, she'd been running the tobacconist's shop for twenty-two years now to the satisfaction of the inhabitants of the administrative districts of Vienna 4 and Vienna 5, you couldn't unexpectedly confront those people with such a drastic change as the closure of their tobacconist's shop, even temporarily, to which I said that in principle, if it was really urgent, I'd be happy to stand in for her in the shop, although only if my own state of health allowed, and my health, as she knew, was almost always poor. Then, looking around, I asked where her husband was, because normally, as I said, her husband helped out behind the counter. Oh, but surely I knew, cried the lady in the tobacconist's, looking at me in surprise, surely I knew her husband was disabled, a tragedy in one way, of course, but lucky in another because it he hadn't been disabled he'd have had considerably less chance of getting the tobacconist's, since the disabled, particularly if disabled in the war, were given strong preference over healthy folk in the allocation of franchises for tobacconist's shops, which after all were a monopoly of the Austrian state. Cold, wet late-autumn weather like this was the worst possible thing for her husband, the weather around All Saints' Day always gave her husband phantom pain in his lower leg, so unfortunately missing, and forced him to take to his bed.

By now I had recovered slightly, and since in the circumstances I saw no chance of describing my bronchial catarrh at greater length and the lady in the tobacconist's made no move to offer me the little folding chair to sit on, I said goodbye and left the place in some haste, a haste

I regretted after struggling on another ten meters or so against the wind, when I noted, to my dismay, that I'd left my pure hand-spun wool scarf behind in the tobacconist's, a slip of the mind that could have serious consequences in this kind of weather. I immediately turned my coat collar right up to my chin and retraced my steps, to find the lady in the tobacconist's shop already waiting for me with the snow-white scarf I'd knitted myself in moss stitch, and I wrapped this item of clothing, which I treasured, round my neck three times and closed the door of the tobacconist's behind me again. I could expect a deterioration in my condition, since through my own stupid carelessness my windpipe had been exposed entirely unprotected to the wind and weather, and I could already feel a distinct constriction in that area, so I made haste to get back to the Death House before I was totally exhausted by my difficulty in breathing.

As I was climbing upstairs, clinging to the banisters, I met my neighbor, a nice woman who used to be a church pastoral assistant and has family living in the attractive Bucklige Welt countryside area of Lower Austria. She very kindly sometimes brings me back a jar of lime-flower honey from her brother-in-law's apiary and queen-bee breeding farm, organic lime-flower honey undamaged by pasteurization is one of the best of medicines for sensitive bronchial tubes, very soothing to people who get attacks of coughing. Fräulein Haslinger looked at me in alarm, asked if I was all right, and helpfully offered me her arm, which I took with relief, and then she led me to my apartment next door to the room where Schubert had died and helped me to open the front door. I thanked her, closed the door, and lay down on my bed without removing my coat and scarf.

Sometimes I wonder what I did to deserve being brought into this world so ill-equipped for the battle of life. I was always sickly. While other children flew high in the air on the swings in the playground, rushed squealing down the slide, clambered rung by rung up the climbing frame and ran tirelessly after shuttlecocks, I would sit listlessly on a bench at the side of the playground, wrapped up in a woolly rug by my mother and not yet entirely recovered from a painful attack of inflammation of the middle ear. And while I listened to the carefree cries of neighboring children playing volleyball on the grass outside the building, all they could hear from me was convulsive coughing from my room on the ground floor when I was in the throes of a violent attack of whooping cough. I can imagine how difficult it must have been for my mother, herself rather fragile, to bring up a child as delicate as I was, in the absence of a father. Although she was naturally melancholy and subject to frequent mood swings, no doubt because of her outstanding artistic talent, she did what she could to cheer me during my periods of sickness, which often went on for weeks. As a trained pianist, she tried to hasten my recovery through the art that meant so much to her. If I was in bed with swollen tonsils and a high fever because of a sudden drop in the temperature, she would sit at the piano and play me songs by her favorite composer Gustav Mahler, particularly the *Kindertotenlieder*, which she loved. Those songs, she used to say, were the tenderest things Mahler ever wrote, so very tender, lyrical and full of tragic premonition. As she played the introduction to the last song, she murmured *sempre molto espressivo*, then looked sorrowfully at me and began intoning, in her dark mezzo-soprano, "With stormy weather and wind about, / I would never have let the children go out, / But oh, they were carried, were carried away." And bringing me a hot lemon drink in bed, she would sing softly, "Ah, too quickly, too soon extinguished light of joy, extinguished light of joy."

My mother was firmly convinced of the healing powers of music, in fact so firmly convinced that she thought traditional medicine unnecessary. If lovely songs don't cure you then antibiotics won't make you better either, she said; codeine and penicillin are not going to succeed where Schönberg and Berg have failed. When the lady who lived above us and felt bothered by both my mother's piano playing and my own persistent coughing, which could easily be heard through all the walls, came to our door with some Ems Salts, my mother said no thank you, not without politely suggesting that hard as it might be for lay people to imagine such a thing, it could still be annoying for a sensitive pianist kept out of the concert hall only by bad luck of the most fateful kind to have her concentration on the dense thematic structure of the piano accompaniment of a Hugo Wolf song disturbed by her neighbor's ringing of the doorbell. And when the neighbor said she wasn't interested in Hugo Wolf, she was just afraid the poor child might choke to death in one of his coughing fits, my mother said sharply that the methods used to treat me could be left to her, my mother, whose right it was to bring me up. And when, at this, the neighbor turned away, sighing, my mother called after her that the usual medicaments you could buy killed far more people than they cured, it was a well-known fact, and she for one would rather not subject her child's growing and therefore very vulnerable organism to the influence of strong doses of Ems Salts and other medicinal drugs, preferring gender methods in line with her little boy's gentle nature. And what could be gentler than music therapy? She could well believe that a woman like her, our neighbor, born and bred the daughter of a working man who lived in Ottakring, a woman who hadn't gone beyond the eight years of compulsory state schooling, had never heard of music therapy, the art of healing through the influence of music on the mind, but it was well known that David, a character in the Old Testament, had cured people by playing the harp, and Orpheus, a name with which she, our neighbor, was unlikely to be familiar, had even snatched his dead wife back from the god of the underworld by the power of his singing. The beneficial power of music had been successfully tested on countless schizophrenics, stammerers, insomniacs and people suffering from war trauma, so did she really think her Ems Salts were on a par with the greatest of all the arts? Our neighbor, who by now had reached the half-landing between our two floors, said a few more things, which I didn't understand apart from a few disquieting words such as custody, irresponsibility and child abuse, whereupon my mother closed the door and sat down at the baby grand again, shaking her head.

I dwelled on such thoughts of my childhood, a sad one clouded by illness, yet also happy because it was irradiated by the unique personality of my dear mother, as I lay in

my coat and scarf on the bedspread I had crocheted out
of remnants of wool during the forced inactivity of a long
period of convalescence. I would have liked to indulge my
memories longer, but I had decided to hang some damp
sheets up in the room to humidify the air by evaporation
and thus relieve my inflamed bronchial tubes, so I got
up and took off my scarf and coat, and although I was a
little dizzy I found my Swiss-made stepladder, stretched a
washing line right across the living room, hung three white
linen sheets on it, and after that I really did soon feel some
relief. Encouraged by this improvement in my condition,
I went into the kitchen and began making the beef broth.
I quickly browned all the ingredients except the beef in a
large pan, added water and salt, and once the liquid began
to boil I added the meat and let it all simmer over very
slow heat, so that there was soon a pleasing aroma in the
flat, reviving me sufficiently to sit at the piano and venture
on playing the song "The Hurdy-Gurdy Man" from Schubert's *Winterreise*. I'd loved this song, with its heartrend-
ing text, ever since my mother played it to me while I was
suffering from diphtheria. At the time, the doctor claimed
my childish larynx was already affected, and he strongly
advised several weeks in a clinic, to which my mother
quite rightly objected that the invisible notes of Schubert,
that most spiritual of all the Viennese composers, would
certainly do more to cure my pharyngeal and tracheal area
than time spent with a set of invalids who were strangers to
me, among overworked nursing staff and in a non-musical
environment. It is from this decision of my mother's that I
date my love of Schubert, a love that has never diminished
but has grown ever stronger in intensity year by year, and

in view of its warmth and tenderness can be compared only with my feelings for my mother herself. I picked up the battered Volume One of the Schubert album for voice and pianoforte accompaniment published by Anton Rück-auf, newly revised and printed with additional expression marks, opened it, and abandoned myself entirely to the song: "There beyond the village the hurdy-gurdy man / With his frozen fingers plays as best he can. / Barefoot on the ice he totters to and fro, / Not a single coin in his dish will go. / No one wants to hear him, no one's eyes will scan / Him, and all the dogs growl at the poor old man." As usual, I felt a spiritual affinity with this pitiful figure, as susceptible as I am to cold winter weather, still turning his hurdy-gurdy to give other people pleasure despite the danger of contracting a severe cold, in fact even catching his death of it. The second half of the song always reduced me to tears while I had diphtheria, which my mother took as a certain sign of the efficacy of Schubert's music and my imminent cure: "So he lets the world go by, go by as it will / And his hurdy-gurdy never once is still. / Strange old music-maker, shall I go with you? / Will you play your music for my own songs too?" In my feverish delirium I followed the shadowy figure of the old man further and further out on the ice. I would have liked to sing the words as I played, but that was naturally impossible, since my bronchial catarrh had a devastating effect on the state of my larynx, my glottis and my vocal cords. To enjoy the song properly, however, I rose from the piano stool and put on the LP of Hans Hotter singing the *Winterreise*, an old recording made in 1942, but of remarkably good quality.

Schubert. He and my mother made life bearable for me, and once I begin to love a human being I am very faithful and seek that person's company as often and as much as I can. The fact that Schubert died on 19 November 1828, one hundred and forty years before my own birth, didn't really make much difference to my efforts. As soon as I realized how strongly I felt about him, I began visiting those places in Vienna which he had frequented during his short life, in the firm belief that his spirit must linger there. First I did some research into the location of the inns and cafés where Schubert used to go with his friends, the Café Bogner in Singerstrasse, the Café Hugelmann on the bank of the Danube, the Oak and Starr inns, the Hungarian Crown, the Green Huntsman and the Red Rooster, the Wolf Preaching to the Geese in Wallnergasse, the Green Anchor in Grünangergasse and the Red Cross on Himmelpfortgrund. Only the Green Anchor Restaurant was still in existence, and the proprietor, a very pleasant man, claimed credibly enough that Schubert had frequently eaten and drunk there over a period of two years, so I ate lunch at the Green Anchor for months on end out of fellow feeling, a habit that finally led to an attack of gastritis. Even more interesting than the inns and cafés were the buildings in which he had lived, particularly the house where he was born at 54 Nussdorferstrasse, known as the Red Crayfish, which today contains a museum, but I also sought out the building at 9 Spiegelgasse in the center of the city, to which Franz von Schober often welcomed his friend, and inquired about the apartments in Tuchlauben and Wipplingerstrasse where the composer had also spent a considerable amount of time, and as the years passed by

I redoubled my efforts to move into one of those apartments, or at least into one of the buildings. The folder in which I filed my correspondence with the owners and tenants of these apartments and buildings and with the Vienna City Council still bears witness to the difficulties with which I had to contend. My dearest wish would have been to live in the building where Schubert was born, but owing to the City Council's lack of understanding I soon realized this was an impossible aim, and my persistent attempts to rent a place in 9 Spiegelgasse, where Schubert had composed the Symphony in B Minor, the Unfinished, weren't as successful as I had hoped. Renting a place in 6 Kettenbrückengasse, known as the Death House, did not at first seem to me particularly desirable, for the simple reason that the place was linked to an irreplaceable loss for mankind, and consequently I feared that living long-term in that fateful spot might further reinforce my tendency to melancholy, probably inherited from my mother and manifesting itself more particularly in the cold months of the year in the form of depression, a fear which I'm happy to say has turned out to be only partly justified.

When all my attempts to live where Schubert had lived had come to nothing, I decided to find out about the Death House after all, and on the occasion of a visit to the room on the second floor where Schubert had died I asked the lady who sat there, knitting with great concentration and selling tickets, who owned the building, to which she replied that these were all council apartments, and then immediately put her tongue firmly between her lips again, for she was obviously engaged in the rather tricky business of turning the heel of a pale blue woolly sock.

Nonetheless, I ventured another question—did she know if one of these apartments might fall vacant in the near future?—and she looked at me suspiciously, returned her tongue to the inside of her mouth and said that as far as she knew the Turkish family of seven living in the three-roomed apartment right next to this room, Schubert's death chamber, was to be evicted in the course of the next six months because the head of the household, who sold fruit and vegetables in the Naschmarkt, was so far behind with his rent, and what's more the tenants' association had unanimously spoken out against the affront of having members of a foreign ethnic group constantly present in Schubert's Death House, in view of the fact that Schubert wrote music that was so very German, so profoundly German. I thanked her for the information and asked her to sell me an entrance ticket, a request with which, after casting me another suspicious glance, the lady complied. I stood in the death chamber for a long time, gazing at a lock of Schubert's hair in a locket and a silver toothpick the composer himself had used, and then listened through headphones to the Sanctus and Benedictus from the E Flat Major Mass, and tried to hide my inner emotion when I went out again past the knitting lady, who now seemed to have mastered the difficulties of the heel, since she was sitting there looking very relaxed.

Soon afterward I visited the Vienna 5 Accommodation Advice Bureau on the second floor of 54 Schönbrunnerstrasse, door 18, and told the clerk on duty that I'd heard, from a reliable source, that a council apartment might soon fall vacant on the second floor of Schubert's Death House at 6 Kettenbrückengasse, as a result of an eviction, and as I had the deepest veneration for Schubert as both a composer and a human being I would very much like to move into the building where he died. The clerk, a remarkably stout young man with sparse fair hair and a thin, reddish moustache, looked me up and down and then asked if my circumstances justified my applying for a council apartment, not everyone in Vienna had the prospect of getting a council apartment, it was a privilege reserved for only a few, and the selection criteria were rigorous. I apologized for my ignorance and said, well then, what *were* the selection criteria, whereupon the clerk inspected me thoughtfully again, twirling the left-hand side of his moustache, and said that I'd have to prove that the state of the place where I was living at present had already impaired my health. When I made haste to say that I'd been unusually susceptible to illness since early childhood, the clerk became rather impatient and said my only chance was to show I lived in a damp basement apartment without its own toilet and had to use one out in the corridor, and that I suffered from severe arthritis as a direct result of living in such conditions, to which I replied, rather discouraged, that unfortunately I was living in my mother's large, comfortably furnished four-roomed apartment near the Church of Maria am Gestade in Vienna 1 and couldn't fulfill either of those stipulations. In that case, said the clerk, leaning back, in that case he could only advise me to rent a place for a while of the kind he had described, and then reapply, showing unmistakable symptoms of arthritis, and if my veneration for Schubert was really as great as I said, he was sure I could make that small sacrifice.

On the way back to my mother's apartment in the little street called Stoss-im-Himmel near the Church of Maria am Gestade, the advice of the clerk in the Accommodation Advice Bureau kept running through my head. His were terrible demands. Delicate from early childhood as I already was, must I deliberately move into a place injurious to my health in order to get the council apartment I longed for in Schubert's Death House? That was not, as he claimed, a small sacrifice but a superhuman one. Such a step could lead to my early death, and I didn't want to emulate the composer in that respect, since I had pupils who needed me. On the other hand, the prospect of living in Schubert's own aura was tempting. As I climbed the stairs to my mother's apartment I decided to discuss the problem with her—a woman with so much experience of life, such perspicacity, such a sense of realism. She did not disappoint me.

My dear child, she said, I've always been anxious to pass on to you the love of music that, as you know, fills every fiber of my being, and I have every reason to suppose that I have achieved that aim in your upbringing. Of course health is a very precious thing, undeniably we must do all we can to preserve it, and for you in particular even greater caution than usual is advisable, since yours is a delicate constitution. However, sometimes an extraordinary chain of circumstances can lead to a situation where considerations of physical well-being must take second place to some higher endeavor. If ideals are involved, and in the case you describe they undoubtedly are, the consistent pursuit of those ideals demands the commitment of one's entire person, even one's life. You mustn't think I shall find it easy to go on living here without your familiar presence, but calling on my maternal authority, which, as you know, is something I seldom do, I advise you—no, I require you—to make the sacrifice of living under insalubrious conditions for a while, for the sake of Franz Peter Schubert. You will be amply recompensed for this sacrifice by the good fortune of knowing yourself, later, to be always in his spiritual presence.

I looked at my mother standing there before me, very upright, one hand laid on the black lacquer lid of the baby grand. What a woman!

So it was that I spent the next few months in a one-roomed basement apartment on the Lerchenfelder Gürtel, with mold creeping up its walls. The desired symptoms set in within a gratifyingly short space of time: first fatigue and loss of appetite, then swelling of my joints and lymph glands, slight distortion and stiffness of my hands and feet, and the appearance of several rheumatic nodes, and when I had also contracted synovial bursal inflammation of the right shoulder because of the damp in the basement flat, I thought the time had come for another application to the Accommodation Advice Bureau. I got my mother's doctor to make out a certificate and went off to Room 18 in search of the stout clerk, who seemed to be impressed by both my sickly appearance and the medical certificate, and promised to support my application.

In this way the knitting lady, the stout clerk and my mother helped me to realize the dream of my life. I have lived in the building where Schubert died for over three years now, and I've never regretted taking the step I did. The quarter is a pleasant one, I can easily get all the provisions I need in the Naschmarkt, the St Mary Magdalene Pharmacy is reassuringly close, the proprietor and proprietress of the Café Anzengruber and the Golden Bell Restaurant like a chat with me, and the other tenants in the building are quiet, friendly people who, I am glad to say, don't seem to mind the sound of singing and the piano that go with my profession.

By now the beef broth was ready, and I drank two good bowls of it, then swallowed the requisite amount of *atropinum* and *arsenicum* pills and made myself a large cup of violet-leaf tea, and before I went to bed I took a bath with the water at body heat, adding a few drops of oil of thyme. Just before lying down I decided to make a hot compress for my chest, to be on the safe side, since my temperature had dropped slightly but was still above normal, and to help me get to sleep I played part of Brahms's *German Requiem*, a choral work said to have been written by the composer in memory of his dead mother. I fell asleep in a mood of cheerful relaxation, not without including my mother and Schubert affectionately in my thoughts first.

But once again my mother wasn't going to let me have a good night's sleep. The terrible nightmare that had plagued me so often recently came back. I was standing in a dark cemetery beside her last resting place, and I heard a hollow voice call: Dig me up, dig me up! I began digging in the hard, black earth with my bare hands until my fingernails broke. Faster, called the menacing voice, faster, my child! I dug and dug until two hands came into view, two dreadful hands, their yellowish bone structure exposed but still partly covered by blackish-brown scraps of skin and flesh. These hands reached out for my snow-white pure wool scarf, which was wound three times round my neck, and began pulling the ends of it tighter and tighter, until I thought I would choke. Come, my child, called the voice, it is quiet here, it is good here! Normally I would wake up at this point, bathed in sweat, and it would take me some time to recover from the nightmare. I never tried defending myself against my mother's hands. But tonight the dream took a new turn; before the hands could seize my scarf I tore it from my neck and threw it in the hole I had just dug. Leave me alone, I cried, find someone else to share your eternal rest! At this my mother rose entirely from her grave, half decomposed, a terrible sight, and grew taller and taller until she was towering high above me. She picked me up with her huge hand of worm-eaten flesh and porous bones, raised me to the level of the black holes that were once her eyes, and then opened her skeletal yellow jaws to swallow me. But before her teeth crushed me I woke with a shriek. It was three thirty-three in the morning. I was trembling all over.

I couldn't understand my dear mother's ghastly behaviour. She was dead, of course she was, she'd died on 28 December three years ago, Holy Innocents' Day. Her mortal remains were buried in a grave in Vienna Central Cemetery, and I took the 71 tram there at least twice a week to talk to her. How could she repay such devotion, enduring even beyond death, in such a disgraceful way? I'd put up with my nightmares for a long time, feeling defenseless and incapable of protest, like a small child. I was surprised by my own untypical conduct in the dream from which I had just woken, by my conspicuous lack of respect for my late beloved mother, but on the other hand

I was gradually beginning to lose patience with the selfish, unloving conduct of the dear departed, and I decided to ask her to explain herself when I next visited the Central Cemetery. And my next visit would be on the very day that had begun three hours thirty-three minutes ago, All Souls' Day, a very suitable date for such a confrontation. After these reflections, I managed to fall asleep again remarkably quickly.

Translated by Anthea Bell

DONALD G. DAVIAU, author, editor, and translator, is Professor of Austrian and German Literature at the University of California, Riverside (emeritus), former editor of the scholarly journal *Modern Austrian Literature* (1974–2000), cofounder and editor of Ariadne Press (1985–1999) devoted to Austrian literature, organizer of the Riverside Annual Austrian Symposium (1983–1999), president of the American Council for the Study of Austrian Literature (1985–2000), and English editor of the electronic journal *TRANS* (1995–).

Daviau is the author and editor of 21 books and 190 articles on such authors as Thomas Bernhard, Max Brod, Arthur Schnitzler, Peter Turrini, and Ernst Weiss, and themes such as Austrian literary history, the reception of Austrian literature in the United States, the image of America in Austrian literature, the question of Austrian identity, Austrian literature in film, and Austrian writers of diaries. His translations include both literary and scholarly texts. He was awarded the prestigious Austrian Ehrenkreuz für Kunst und Wissenschaft in 1979.

He lives in Riverside, California, when he is not in Austria.

Franz Kafka's "A Hunger Artist" was translated by Ian Johnston and reprinted here, with minor modifications, by permission of the translator.

Robert Musil's "The Man Without Qualities" is excerpted from chapters 39 and 40 from the book of the same name. Translated by Eithne Wilkins and Ernst Kaiser, © 1953, published by Coward-McCann, Inc.

Elias Canetti's "The Red Cock" was originally published in *Auto da Fe,* published by Random House, English translation © 1946 C. V. Wedgwood. Reprinted by permission of Random House, U.K.

Peter Henisch's "Negatives of My Father" (from the novel of the same name) was published by Ariadne Press. English translation © 1990 Anne Close Ulmer. Reprinted by permission of Ariadne Press.

Heimito von Doderer's "The Studlhof Steps" was originally published in *Relationships: An Anthology of Contemporary Austrian Prose,* edited by Adolph Opel, published by Ariadne Press. English translation © 1991 Gudrun Gomori and Barbara Marshall. Reprinted by permission of Ariadne Press.

Lilian Faschinger's "Vienna Passion" is excerpted from the first chapter of *Vienna Passion,* English translation © 2000 Anthea Bell, published by Headline Books.

Ingeborg Bachmann's "Sightseeing in an Old City" was originally published in *Austrian Identities: Twentieth-Century Short Fiction,* edited by Craig Decker, published by Ariadne Press. English translation © 2004 Margaret McCarthy. Reprinted by permission of Ariadne Press.

Erich Wolfgang Skwara's "Visit to Vienna" was originally published in *Relationships: An Anthology of Contemporary Austrian Prose,* edited by Adolph Opel, published by Ariadne Press. English translation © 1991 Harvey I. Dunkle. Reprinted by permission of Ariadne Press.